Praise for
Cloud Accounting

"In a world of fast moving technology, Cloud Accounting offers practical, straight forward guidance to businesses on how to harness this technology to move their businesses forward. A 'must have' for businesses in growth mode."

Susan Thompson
Partner Marketing Manager-East Region-Microsoft Dynamics
Microsoft Corporation

"With close to 30 years of experience in the ERP Business, I've seen less than a handful of changes that have significantly impacted the customer. The cloud will be a game changer for both the customers who buy it and the vendors who sell it. And while no one knows with 100% accuracy exactly what the future entails, Cloud Accounting hits the nail square on the head with a logical, easy to follow methodology to help you figure out what it may or may not mean to your company. ANY executive thinking that there has to be a better answer to corporate business systems than spreadsheet hell and basic accounting will find that this book saves them countless hours, monumental distractions from their business and many sleepless nights. Well worth the time it takes to read."

Bruce Ciarleglio, Consultant
Salesworks

"This is a highly helpful guide for any business who is weighing the many ERP deployment options available. Readers can easily connect with the real world personas and business situations provided within, making cloud computing easily digestible by business executives who are not technologists by trade. This is a must read for anyone about to participate or lead an ERP evaluation."

Christine Zmuda
Director of ERP and Partner Strategy
Microsoft Corporation

"Bill and SSi Consulting have offered cloud solutions to their customers for years. In this book, he and David Russell lay out an engaging story of customers navigating their business systems to the cloud. This book will help anyone faced with the choice of keeping their business software on premise or in the cloud. As the 'cloud' has become a normal part of our everyday lives – this book will certainly come in handy for any firms looking at making a move to the ever expanding cloud."

Sam Cool, Vice President
Planet Technologies

"This book makes it FUN to learn about cloud computing. The characters in the fable let you see things from all sides, and acknowledge both the logic and emotion that goes into making a change. The ending switches to a bullet point style if you prefer to learn what you need to know in a nutshell. If you are choosing what's next for your accounting systems, read this book first."

Diane Gasal
Professional Certified Coach

Cloud Accounting

From Spreadsheet Misery to Affordable Cloud ERP

William Aiton and David Russell

Smyth Barnabas Publishing
www.SmythBarnabas.com

Please note that much of this publication is based on personal experience and anecdotal evidence. Although the authors and publisher have made every reasonable attempt to achieve complete accuracy of the content in this Book, they assume no responsibility for errors or omissions. Also, you should use this information as you see fit, and at your own risk. Your particular situation may not be exactly suited to the examples illustrated here; in fact, it is likely that they are not the same, and you should adjust your use of the information and recommendations accordingly.

Any trademarks, service marks, product names or named features are assumed to be the property of their respective owners, and are used only for reference. There is no implied endorsement if we use one of these terms.

Printed in the United States of America
First Printing: November 2011.

Cover design by David Reyes.
Editing by Brandon Hoye

Library of Congress Copyright Registration #: 1-675184671
Writers Guild of America Intellectual Property Registry: 1539222
13-digit ISBN: 978-0-9771659-8-8
10-digit ISBN: 0-9771659-8-1

DISCLAIMER: The contents of this Book are intended for general information purposes only. Information contained in this document is not intended to be a substitute for legal advice or to provide legal guidance of any kind whatsoever. If legal advice or other expert assistance is required, the services of a competent professional should be sought.

For additional information visit:

www.SSiConsulting.com

www.SuccessWithPeople.com

www.SmythBarnabas.com

Contents

Chapter 1

Analysis

Paralysis

"What the HELL is going on over there?!"

James tilted the phone away for the sake of his eardrums. He promised to resolve the problem first thing tomorrow and apologized for the error. After a few more choice words the irate contracting agent hung-up. This brought the number of emotionally upset clients to three for the month.

As CEO and founder of a consulting firm serving government agencies, James had been instrumental in helping the company achieve its recent unprecedented success. Even though the firm was growing steadily, James still preferred to give clients his direct number so he could learn about problems first-hand when they occurred.

The mounting number of angry calls signaled that James and his employees were starting to lose control of the business. Their small business accounting program and practice of using spreadsheets to manage projects and costs was buckling under the strain of an increased client load. If the problems continued, they could destroy the company:

- Projects were going over budget due to the company's inability to track all of its expenditures.

- Unanticipated invoices were submitted to James from both VARs (Value Added Resellers) and sub-contractors.

- Expense reports were not submitted on a timely basis, nor consistently entered into their small business accounting program.

- The company did not have enough up-to-date data to support change-orders before the work was done.

As James walked to his car, he thought about his two kids and the college visits they had made this past summer. The increased revenue of recent months had seemed like a lock to help pay for their tuition.

Now James knew if amicable client agreements continued to morph into disgruntled clients then things would get ugly, and cancelled contracts would be all that was left to pay those huge tuition bills.

The company needed to scale its work more efficiently and effectively.

James started the car and began driving towards a board meeting across town. Volunteering to be on the board for a local non-profit had been Esther's idea three years ago. A fellow CEO of a local software development firm and friendly competitor, the two executives had attended the same university and remained friends ever since.

While at school, James had asked Esther out on one awkward date. In the process he introduced her to her future husband, Dan, who was James' best friend. James would eventually meet and marry Bridgette, a friend of Esther's, and the two families would remain close.

Administratively, Esther was the salt to James' pepper, which worked wonders during board meetings. Whereas James would challenge each statement to drill down on additional detail, Esther focused on summary data and drove discussions to an agreement of actions that led to measurable results.

As a highly detail-oriented introvert, James preferred postponing decisions and tended to suffer from "analysis paralysis." Esther was the polar opposite. She was a vibrant people-person who loved taking on problems and looked beyond the details to how solutions would positively affect outcomes. James put it another way. He privately joked to Esther and Dan that she would not know a detail if it hit her in the face.

In reality, James and Esther balanced each other so well they became somewhat professionally dependent on one another. They would use each other as sounding boards for their ideas and accountability partners to make certain they followed through on key initiatives. Their in-person meetings would occur over coffee with Peter, the executive of the non-profit on whose board they both served, after their monthly board meetings.

James liked hearing Esther's ideas on how to move things ahead. Balancing her encouragement to "go for it" with his analysis helped James more than once make decisions he had been delaying. Esther saw these conversations as opportunities to test her ideas on James and Peters' skeptical minds so she could lower the risk of her initiatives.

They joked about competing with one another, but the real value of Esther and James' relationship was an ability to make better decisions because of their respect for each other's differences.

James continued to think as he turned into the non-profit's parking lot. *Our company needs to quickly find a better way to manage the costs of our projects. If we do not fix the problems soon, then upset clients would lead to lost contracts, failure to meet government regulations, and an end to our recent rapid growth... or worse.*

Chapter 2

Fails with
Details

"How many hours? There's no way he worked that many... he took a day off last week."

On the way to her car Esther was already back on the phone with her office, dealing with timecard issues. Her company was growing by leaps and bounds. Unfortunately growing to over 50 people was causing the software development company's small business accounting program to burst at the seams:

- Due to inefficient reminders and management checks, employees often forgot or procrastinated recording their hours worked on their spreadsheets until the end of the week. As a result, employees often guessed and recorded hours incorrectly on a weekly basis instead of accurately on the day the work was done.

- Expenses were not properly assigned to the correct department because those spreadsheets could not be integrated with the company's small business accounting program.

- The tracking of hours and work done by sub-contractors could not be properly integrated nor consistently tracked with the company's present software.

The company was hemorrhaging money due to these inefficient processes and its back office software. As a result, profits were dropping even though the firm was growing.

Esther loved facing problems head on. As a verbally outgoing and persuasive person, she could be thrown into a group of people and become everyone's best friend in a matter of minutes (and forget all their names five minutes later). Juxtaposed to James, she was an extrovert who tended to miss details. She made up for this weakness by hiring people who naturally caught things she overlooked. She valued achieving results, learning, and finding better ways to do things.

This is why her company's consistent problems with their accounting software infuriated Esther. She enjoyed problem solving, but what was the point of growing rapidly if your profits could not expand with your company?

Esther continued to think as she took the exit off the freeway. She looked forward to discussing this problem with James and Peter over coffee after their board meeting. Esther knew James' company was growing like hers. She wondered if James was experiencing similar headaches and had possibly come up with any solutions.

Esther sighed as she parked her car and started walking towards the non-profit's offices. It frustrated her that she could not resolve this problem immediately herself. As iron sharpens iron, the only comfort Esther had was that her ideas often became more defined and she made better decisions after talking with James and Peter to draw-out more details.

Esther thought about why she needed a solution fast. *If we can't find effective methods for tracking hours logged by employees and sub-contractors, it's going to be more difficult to turn a profit, fund company growth, and maintain the trust it took us years to develop with clients. Without a solution we're headed for a brick wall... if not a cliff.*

Chapter 3

No Driving

As James entered the conference room, the first person he saw was Peter, chatting with another board member a few seats down the table. James went over to say hello.

"Hi, Peter," said James, extending his hand.

Peter took the hand, said one last comment to the board member sitting next to him and turned to James.

"James! Hello! How are you?"

"Doing alright," replied James as he nodded to the other board member. "Company's keeping me on my toes, as usual."

"Of course," said Peter. "Are we still on for coffee after this?"

James nodded. "I believe so."

"Excellent. Will Esther be able to make it?"

"I think so. I haven't talked to her this week, but I haven't heard anything to the contrary. I'll bet she's just running a bit late."

James' prediction turned out to be true. As the board started reviewing the agenda for the meeting, Esther slipped in and joined the others around the conference table.

Since Esther's office was located furthest from the non-profit's headquarters, they were accustomed to Esther joining them around agenda review time. Even Esther's apologetic small wave towards Peter had become customary. He waved back and she settled in for business as usual.

Except... as the meeting continued, he realized something was off. James could not quite put his finger on it, but he knew this meeting felt significantly different than the ones in the past.

The meeting was primarily reviewing three initiatives of the growing non-profit and the overall status of the organization. James looked from one member to the next, trying to pinpoint what was out of place.

Another board member expressed his feelings on a certain question. Esther smiled once he was finished and looked back at her laptop.

There it was. Smiling looks and encouraging nods had replaced Esther's usual routine of speaking out with passionate feelings on each subject and driving discussions to decisions. Without Esther's active participation in the conversation, the meeting had turned into a "feelings fest," with members expressing their opinions, but no conclusive decisions being reached.

James realized something else. He was not fully engaged either. Typically he would be drawing out the details and challenging people to prove their points. Unfortunately he was distracted by his own problems. He had to figure out how to fix their processes for job costing.

I can get Esther's opinion after the meeting, thought James. *Maybe not, though. She seems pretty distracted. I wonder if she closed another big piece of business.*

Distracted

Roughly halfway through the meeting, Esther noticed something was wrong. It took her a few minutes, but she realized James seemed very distracted. Usually he was a pit bull demanding details and justification as people made proposals.

Today he was observing with a distant look in his face and his questions were sparse.

As she listened to the group talk more it became clear there was another problem. Without her driving discussions to a conclusion the meeting was incredibly boring. People kept repeating each other rather than adding something valuable to the discussion.

However she could not get her company problems out of her mind.

She had tried bribing her techs to enter their time every two hours or at least on a daily basis. She had offered other rewards. She had threatened them. Nothing worked and the company's system for managing their time stunk.

It was then that she remembered James had talked her out of updating their software a year ago. His firm has been growing, so his way of managing projects must be flawless.

I'll have to pick his brain today, thought Esther. *He sure seems distracted though... maybe he landed a big new contract.*

Chapter 5

Not

Alone

The meeting was moving along at a sluggish pace, but that was the least of Peter's problems right now. As the executive of the non-profit, Peter was preoccupied by thoughts of the problems challenging his organization because of its growth. Although expanding their impact was a good problem to have, it was a problem nonetheless.

They had been fortunate to get several new grants recently, but they manage the requirements in spreadsheets and it was becoming time consuming, prone to error and lacking an effective way to confirm the data was complete or accurate.

In addition to this spreadsheet hell they were stuck in, the organization had three different software products: One for managing donor information, a small business accounting program, and another to manage projects. This made it increasingly difficult to produce the reports needed to manage the organization.

These delays and reporting errors could soon put the organization out of compliance with regulatory and external audit requirements. This could make them ineligible to apply for any more grants.

Due to other priorities, Peter had not been able to investigate ways to resolve the situation. Because he was hired to deliver solutions, not problems, Peter was not prepared to share his concerns with the board just yet. Unfortunately the need for resolution was increasing daily.

"Alright," cut in Peter. "Our time is almost up. We need to finish these discussions and define the action items to complete prior to our next board meeting."

As ideas were volleyed back and forth across the conference room, Peter noticed two voices suspiciously silent from the conversation.

Esther and James, usually two of the most vocal members, remained uncharacteristically quiet. They were observing and nodding their way through each debate rather than actively participating.

This was really odd. From a business perspective Esther was the "ping" to James' "pong." Without them, the board meeting had no game. The back and forth debate necessary to hammer out solutions and make progress was missing. The other board members were just tossing around their ideas and not really listening to one another. No one drilled down on detail. Everyone was talking but no one was listening. Nothing significant was getting done.

Peter knew James and Esther's companies were experiencing unprecedented success and rapid growth. He wondered if they were just overwhelmed with their business success and distracted with details from their office. Peter was very socially engaging and politically conscious. He sincerely cared about Esther and Peter, yet he also questioned whether their struggles could help him get out of his spreadsheet and small business accounting software hell.

Peter had been hired to help grow the organization and they were going gangbusters. The software to manage the organization could not keep up with its growth. He had planned to discuss his spreadsheet/software issues with

Esther and James during their coffee session after the board meeting, but they seemed preoccupied with problems of their own.

As other board members were pontificating their views, Peter relaxed and realized how much he appreciated Esther and James' involvement in the organization. They were always available as sounding boards for him on any issue. They kept their commitments. Peter also remembered two of the key reasons they had such a productive relationship.

First, Esther and James only shared coffee after the board meetings if Peter came along with them. They did this to avoid the risk of giving the appearance of having a relationship that was beyond business and the friendship of their families. Peter respected this since he had known too many top executives take a different approach and fall to temptation, with catastrophic results for both their families and careers.

Second, Esther and James were wise enough to appreciate their different work behaviors and values rather than let them be a barrier to a mutually beneficial relationship. This enabled them to leverage the natural strengths of each other to make better decisions. They shared ideas openly and fully debated facts, opinions and reactions that more ego-driven executives would never consider. The past three years of post-meeting coffees had given Peter lots of ideas to apply at the non-profit. He also developed similar behaviors with his team, which resulted in greater productivity and higher trust between employees.

Peter had a sense this afternoon's coffee session would be very interesting.

Who knows? Peter thought. *They must have faced issues similar to ours in the past. Maybe their discussion today will help me figure out how to overcome my problem.*

Chapter 6

Misgivings

After the meeting, Esther, James and Peter crossed the street to Java Joe's, their usual haunt. Esther and James' muted behavior during the meeting melted away as they debated who should pay for the coffee.

"I'll pay for it," announced Esther as they stepped onto the sidewalk after crossing the street.

"I don't think so," replied James, holding the door open for the other two. "You paid last month."

"You sure?" Esther asked as she got in line. "I could have sworn you paid. How did you trick me into paying yet thinking you paid? You should be in sales."

Esther and James continued their banter with Peter watching in amusement until they reached the cashier.

"Peter?" Esther implored. "Could you please intervene? It appears we have a stalemate."

Peter smiled. "Oh, I wouldn't worry too much about it…"

"James! Caramel Macchiato!" The girl behind the counter yelled, sliding a cup of frothy, steaming goodness onto the pick-up counter.

James looked puzzled. "That's funny. That's my favorite dri—"

"Esther! Toffee Nut Latte!"

"Huh?" Esther mused. "Mine too."

"Imagine that," said Peter, stepping past them to grab a third cup that slid across the pick-up counter.

Peter started to smirk as they both shook their heads. He had ordered and paid for their drinks on his cell phone before leaving the conference room. After thanks were exchanged and drinks collected, the three found their customary table by the window.

"Well," said Esther, "Everyone seemed to have a lot to say in the meeting today. Wouldn't you agree, James?"

James shrugged, obviously a bit uncomfortable. "I may not be the best person to ask. I was up late night last night."

"I don't buy it," Esther challenged. "When George gives his two cents in meetings, you usually draw at least another dollar out of him. Where were the questions and cross-examinations today? You've been tired for years! What's really going on?"

James fiddled with his coffee cup for a few seconds. "Well, work has been extra stressful recently."

"I thought your business was booming," remarked Peter.

"It has been," agreed James. "The only problem is some of our systems haven't been able to keep up with the growth and it's coming back to bite us."

Esther shifted in her seat. "What systems?"

"Our small business accounting program and spreadsheets specifically," replied James. "We have outgrown their ability to manage accurate, detailed records of our accounts, invoices or expenditures.

"I got cussed out this morning by a contracting agent after we went over budget on their project. I told him we'd fix the problem tomorrow. He's willing to pay for the extra work, but two other clients this month made us eat the errors. I'm not sure how to solve the problem, or prevent it from happening again with the software we've got. Too many details are getting lost or reported inaccurately when it comes to measuring actual costs against budgets for projects."

Esther was frustrated. James apparently did not have the magical fix she needed for her systems, but that was not what upset her. "You are playing the victim now, but you could have avoided this if you followed my advice a year ago to implement more scalable software."

James looked up from his frothy cup of caffeine. His stress was showing. "Our systems were working fine back then. I like to rely on proven products and solutions. Heck, you wanted to be a pioneer in cloud computing. It's still just catching on."

"Yeah, well it couldn't have put you in a worse position," responded Esther. "It was worth the gamble, assuming there are any significant risks to the cloud versus our on-premise solutions. Just look at the business you've gained in the last four months."

James paused for a moment, then looked up and started to work his way out of the corner of this debate.

"What about you?" He replied. "I noticed you nodding today, and smiling. Not much talking, though. Are you feeling alright?"

Esther waves her hand dismissively. "The topics we discussed today weren't really my area of expertise."

James laughed. "As if that's ever stopped you before! My guess is your company's growth is giving you headaches just like mine. How's it going over there?"

Esther smiled. If James had held back in the meeting, he was coming alive now. Being able to verbalize and talk through his concerns must have brought back his competitive spirit.

"Times are tough right now," said Esther, looking Peter and James in the eye. "Business is growing, but we're having trouble with our software as well. In fact, I had to deal with a payroll situation on the way here with an employee who entered hours for a day he had taken off. It turned out to be an honest mistake, but our current system has too many manual processes and opportunities for errors. We've got to find a solution for recording hours worked by employees and to manage our sub-contractors better in order to keep the business profitable."

Esther paused. "Actually James, the more I think about it, the more I realize the need to thank *you* for my problems. *You're* the one that persuaded me to put off upgrading my software a year ago."

James was ready. "Back then neither of us had this much business coming in."

"Oh, baloney! Our growth today is just a continuation of our growth over the last five years. Now we need to get this fixed fast. Otherwise, we can say goodbye to our increased business. Last night I did just a quick search online and found dozens of companies offering alternatives to our small business accounting software and spreadsheet hell. It should take no time at all to find the right one."

James countered. "They all sound great, but what if you pick the wrong one? Why go to the cloud when we might be able to stay with the on-premise solutions our people know how to support?   At least now we know how to use our software. Sure there are problems, but maybe they can be fixed with add-on products to our small business accounting program. This isn't like buying paper cups. I'm not even sure we need a new system. Maybe it's just a factor of my people learning how to deal with the increased workload."

A brief debate ensued, with Esther arguing a cloud solution would make the transition to new software simple, lower costs, and be faster to implement while James countered cloud computing was still in its infancy and too risky.

Looking on, Peter could tell the two were at an impasse. Esther could pick a vendor tomorrow and run with their solution, while James sounded like he would rather hold on to his comfortable, "proven" yet broken system until it killed his company. A compromise had to be reached.

"Alright! Time out!" Peter interjected with a smile. "Let me suggest a compromise."

Esther and James quieted down to listen to the ever-diplomatic Peter. "First of all, let's not lose sight of the fact the only reason you share this big problem is because you are so successful. It may surprise you, but our non-profit has similar problems. We have also outgrown our accounting software so it is in all of our best interests to find a solution." Peter paused for effect, and the new information about the non-profit's problem further caught their attention.

"I propose each of you take the next month to identify and do preliminary interviews with five different companies that you feel can meet your needs. Then, after our next board meeting you can present a one-page summary on each of the top two companies you feel offers the best solutions."

"Sounds reasonable," said Esther.

"Yeah, it's alright with me," echoed James.

Peter was particularly glad Esther and James were fast tracking ways to solve their dilemmas because answers to their problems might help him solve his technology challenges too.

After saying their goodbyes, Peter was deep in thought returning to the office. He wondered how Esther and James would approach the situation. James was a natural skeptic, but Esther was born to sell. Sales people could be the easiest ones to pitch; therefore Esther's quick decision-making style could make her an easy target for a lying sales person.

Then again, if a shrewd sales person sold James a solution based on his fears rather than his true needs, James could be led like a lamb to the slaughter. Peter wondered if they would balance themselves out in this process or just choose to go their separate ways.

Chapter 7

What
Cloud?

As Peter returned to his office he thought less of James and Esther, and more about the technology challenges of his non-profit. It was spreadsheet hell. Maybe his organization's growth could help him purchase a new system and the payback of increased efficiency would reduce his long term overhead.

Without letting his staff know, he had started a process to create a list of what they needed from their accounting and business software to support the continued expansion of the organization.

Angie, his trusted assistant, walked into his office as he logged into his computer. "So how was your meeting?"

"Only okay," Peter replied as he split his attention between checking his email and her question. "James and Esther were distracted because their companies have outgrown their accounting software. As a result they were not as engaged in the meeting so we did not get as much done as I had hoped."

"Well at least it gives you something else in-common with them," responded Angie with a smile. Although the general staff did not know Peter's plans for a massive software upgrade, he trusted her with everything about the organization. "And since you bring up the subject, I have identified two additional things we need from our next generation of business software. Ideally, we would like to:

1. Analyze the delivery of our services and measure attributes of our organizational performance to confirm efficiency and effectiveness.

2. We also need a better way to manage our marketing campaigns so they are targeted more specifically based on donor type, project, and geography.

"I added these to our list. Do you want to review the list again?"

"Yes, this is good timing. Just read it to me," Peter said nodding.

Angie looked at her tablet computer and read, "The other needs on the list are:

3. Centralize all grant-related information to improve tracking, project management and reporting.

4. Integrate data from all of our systems so we can measure and report on anything the organization is doing.

5. Improve service by consolidating member and donor data so staff has complete information from a single system.

6. Find ways to automate and streamline critical business processes to reduce costs, decrease errors and save time so we can achieve more services with the same number of staff.

7. Automate compliance with regulatory and external audit requirements (for example, SFAS 117).

"It sounds like enough to me. Thanks," acknowledged Peter. "I'm confident if we can meet these requirements then the solution will provide other helpful functionality too.

I've got about 30 minutes before my next meeting. Unless you want me for something, I need to better understand the difference between cloud computing and on-premise solutions."

"Go for it. I'll catch up with you later," Angie replied as she turned and left Peter alone to do his research.

Because Esther and James would report on their recommendations in a month, Peter had the luxury of not having to research potential solutions. He just needed to understand the basic differences between the cloud and on-premise solutions so he could comprehend their conclusions. He found his answers quickly.

On-premise solutions have been around for decades. Basically this is where software and data shared by multiple people are loaded onto a server in the same building and accessed by individual computers ("clients"). This was why on-premise solutions were also called "client/server." There were advantages and disadvantages to on-premise solutions. The advantages were:

1. The software applications were easier to maintain because they reside on a single server instead of dozens, hundreds or even thousands of client computers. Maintenance included repairing, upgrading, replacing and even relocating server hardware and software without affecting the client computers. (Cloud solutions share these benefits.)

2. The latest versions of data were also easy to access and update because it resided on the server(s).

3. Critical data was very secure on the server(s) if software and hardware was purchased specifically to protect the server whereas individual client computing

devices such as desktop computers, laptops, and tablet computers lack this level of protection.

4. Servers did most of the calculation work so results were calculated quickly on the client workstations.

The key disadvantages of on-premise solutions were high cost, longer implementation times, slowing data access times as your number of users increase, and the cost to maintain the servers and software. Also, purchasing robust security can be very expensive for smaller organizations like Esther, James and Peter's.

He read about a concern regarding the time it took to access data per on-premise server. Apparently for some companies, data access times can slow significantly as the number of simultaneous client computer requests increase. However this was not an issue for him, James or Esther.

He was surprised to realize the cloud was not as new as James feared. It turned out his non-profit was already using the cloud because their website and email was managed on another company's servers.

The cloud metaphor came from decades of engineers drawing the internet as a cloud. It transferred to this new technology because cloud applications were accessed solely over the internet.

The difference now was more sophisticated applications were moving to the cloud and the hardware components were being designed to scale automatically based on how much capacity was needed. Therefore cloud computing solutions rarely experienced slow access times due to unexpectantly high user demands. Cloud people described this capability as "elasticity," where literally thousands of servers sitting in a hosting facility can be harnessed to meet your momentary needs. *That's a lot cheaper than us buying all that stuff,* Peter thought.

Another financial incentive of cloud computing was tax benefits. It takes years for a company to depreciate the cost of server hardware and software, but cloud computing was a service. This meant 100% of its cost can be expensed the year it was paid. This would lower their tax liability and increase cash flow.

Peter loved the fact that cloud computing was a pay-as-you-go service. His people initially were only using about 10-20% of their server's capacity, except during donor campaigns, so they were wasting 80-90% of the server cost most of the year. Cloud computing enabled him to only pay for the capacity they used and the system automatically expanded (elasticity) when he needed it at a reasonable, temporary cost.

I like this, Peter thought. *The cloud hosting companies replace their hardware systems every three years without any additional costs to us so our ERP system is never running on obsolete hardware.*

The fourth benefit turned out to be all Peter cared to understand about cloud computing for the moment. It was that cloud solutions were faster to plan, purchase, configure or customize, test and roll-out than comparable on-premise solutions.

People were debating whether cloud computing or on-premise solutions were more secure, but Peter decided to leave that debate to James and Esther. He leaned back in his chair to ponder this new information for a moment.

This is cool, he thought. *James and Esther had outgrown their small business accounting program and spreadsheets at the same time as his non-profit. They all now needed to move beyond small business accounting systems to more of an enterprise resource planning solution ("ERP") like major corporations, but designed for small-midsize business. Wow. That sounded scary, but he had two aces "in the hole: James and Esther. And they were going to do the research on his next generation of software for him!*

Chapter 8

Research

The next week, Esther set a meeting with her administrative assistant, Jennifer and controller, Daryl.

Esther had hired her team carefully to balance her natural strengths and business objectives. Because he was an analytical like James, Daryl could irritate her at times as he tried to hold her accountable. As much as she hated his delays to discuss details, systems and skepticism, that was exactly why Esther hired him. Mostly she contained her frustration and appreciated Daryl by reminding herself of the many times his approach had saved them a lot of money and time.

Jennifer, who helped keep her boss focused, naturally provided a more structured, predictable work environment for Esther. She was a sounding board, filter to eliminate unnecessary distractions, and confidant. She could join Daryl in his skepticism, but still supported Esther's push for results.

Just before the meeting, Esther started rummaging around in the top left drawer of her desk for the small box where she kept people's business cards. In it Esther found Marie Arnold's card of KOQB Group. Marie had been the one who motivated Esther a year ago to tell James that they needed to leave their small business accounting software /spreadsheet hell.

Daryl knocked on the open door. "Hi, Esther!"

"Hi, Daryl," replied Esther. "Come on in."

"Thanks."

Daryl made himself comfortable in one of the three chairs in front of Esther's desk.   Jennifer joined them shortly afterwards.

"Well," started Esther. "As you both well know, our small business accounting software is fast becoming obsolete. Daryl, you worked with me yesterday on the issue with Thomas' timesheet and Jennifer, you've worked side-by-side with me through other headaches our software's caused.

"Enough is enough.   Daryl, I want you to research four companies around the area that offer business software alternatives to our small business accounting program. Jennifer, once he selects prospective vendors I want you to set up meetings with their reps within the..."

"Esther?" Daryl slid forward to the edge of his seat.

"...Month. Yeah?"

"I'm excited about where we're going with this, but if you're putting a team together to look at some options, I suggest including John as well. I know he's new to the company and more on the development side of things rather than operations, but his experience evaluating software should help us. Also, it sounds like we are moving from a small business accounting program and spreadsheets to a small-midsize company ERP."

"What's ERP?" Jennifer asked.

"Enterprise Resource Planning software," Daryl replied matter-of-factly. "It basically means software that helps us manage a variety of activities involved in the important parts of our business. For instance, it should help us manage our accounting, contact management, jobs, projects, the hours people work and more, all in one package."

Esther nodded. "That's a great idea, Daryl. Jennifer, will you please see if John can join us?"

Jennifer left to track down the company's CTO. John was the Dr. Jekyll/Mr. Hyde of the team. He was both an analytical and a driver. This meant his natural style was to be a top performer, but he actually balanced the need to deliver results on schedule with a high attention to details. The challenge at times was he could get personally conflicted as part of him wanted to just get something done while another part of him was eager to gather more details or think about it more.

It only took a few minutes to have John join the meeting. "Wow, this sounds great," said John once he was brought up to speed. "Have you come up with a list of what our top needs are for this new software?"

"Not yet," said Esther. "However, now is an excellent time to start."

Over the next hour, the four of them came up with a list of what they need most from their next generation of business management software:

- **Time Management**: Employees must have an effective and user-friendly way to log hours worked into the system.

- **Expense Reports**: A reliable process for accepting, approving, managing and reporting on expense reports by department.

- **Tracking Subs**: A system for tracking the work done by sub-contractors with task assignment, real-time status, billing and reporting options.

- **Client Self-Service**: A simple way for clients to initiate support tickets, view the status of their requests and a comprehensive audit trail of client interactions regarding each ticket.

- **Notifications**: Automated notifications so clients and our employees/managers are notified when tasks are completed or work goes beyond estimates.

- **Project Management**: Track or review the status and details of all active/inactive projects in our portfolio including by defect or enhancement.

- **Reporting**: Compare unbillable versus billable time, overtime, missing time and much more.

- **Task Management**: Assign tasks, track progress toward due dates and report by task—available real-time to approved team members and client contacts.

"Thanks again for taking the lead on this project, John," said Esther. "The four of us will participate in each vendor meeting, but you guys decide on the five vendors we should consider."

Esther picked up the business card she had laying on her desk. "I only ask that you include the KOQB Group in the final group of five companies to present to us. Here is Marie Arnold's business card. They were the first company that approached us a year ago with alternatives to our small business accounting program and I declined. I was very impressed with her company at the time. Let's see what they've got."

"Of course," said Daryl, taking the card. "We have to do some work to identify all possible vendors and narrow it down to five. We can accomplish that by Friday. Then we can schedule two presentations, back-to-back, during weeks two and three, and one the final week. I suggest Tuesday afternoons so we have time to gather any last minute details before your next non-profit board meeting. Does that work for everyone?"

After nods circled the room, Esther moved to close the meeting. "As you know, our profits have slipped despite increasing revenues. I want a solution, the *right* solution, fast. I feel like we're in small business accounting software and spreadsheet hell. I want to get out of it *now*."

Chapter 9

Preparation

James looked down at the small stack of folders organized neatly in front of him on the conference table. His controller, Victor, and vice president of operations, Sally, were seated immediately to his left; his vice president of tech services, Travis, was to his right.

When hiring for these positions, James intentionally found behavioral types to balance his tendency towards analysis paralysis. Victor and Sally's natural strengths were similar to Esther. They helped James keep focused on the "big picture" and make decisions faster rather than get lost in the details. As a highly skeptical analytical, Travis was wired more like James, but he naturally avoided conflict and communicated effectively with others throughout projects.

"The time has come for a change," began James, "As you know, and I expressed to you in my email meeting invite, our small business accounting program is killing us. As much as it pains me to admit, we need to research and implement new business accounting software to support our growth. I hope you all have come to this meeting prepared to define our greatest current and future needs.

"Rather than start with my thoughts, I want to hear from you," he continued, opening and closing the dry marker in his hand as he stood in front of the whiteboard. "We have always been smarter as a team than I have been on my own. I need your help. Each of you has complained about our current system. The sooner we get comfortable with our true needs, the faster we can get this situation resolved. So, how about ladies go first? Sally, what is the critical functionality you want from this new system?"

Over the next half-hour, James and his executive team defined a long list of capabilities their mid-sized project-driven firm wanted from its business management software. At the top of the list were:

1. **Budget Tracking Assistance:** Track all additional purchases made on projects on a real-time basis.

2. **Invoice Management:** Record invoices as they are submitted.

3. **Expense Reporting/Tracking Management:** Submit expense reports and automatically categorize them with the correct department.

4. **Change Order Management:** Track up-to-date data in order to support change-orders before the work is done.

5. **Timesheet Management:** A reliable process for managing timesheets to capture job costs.

6. **Competitive Bid Assistance:** A dependable system for analyzing costs and profits to determine job-cost structures that assist in placing competitive bids for government contracts.

7. **Regulation Compliance Checks:** The software must assist the company in complying with federal accounting regulations, including strict job-costing and timesheet management regulations required by the Federal Acquisition Regulations, supervised by from the Defense Contract Audit Agency (DCAA).

"Good," said James after Victor came up with the seventh point. "Now, let's think to the future. What might we need our system to do in one, two or five years from now?"

"We need it to be scalable," offered Travis. "The company's grown from your one-man operation to about 75 employees. Once we resolve this issue then our growth should even happen faster. Multiple departments and people will need to have access to the business accounting software simultaneously without experiencing longer wait times between screens. Right now, only a limited number of people can access small business accounting program before it noticeably slows down."

Victor also chipped in. "We also need a system without spreadsheets, or one that makes certain we are working on the most recent version. We're getting to the point where we there are literally hundreds of spreadsheets. It's too many to manage. People keep accessing older documents accidentally and updating the wrong versions."

James nodded as he wrote this last idea on the whiteboard with the other most critical needs. He then started passing out the folders that were in front of him, keeping one for himself. "Good. Alright, this is the research I have done on alternatives to our small business accounting program during the last few months. You'll find profiles of five different companies I selected that offer alternatives. These are the solutions we will be considering, unless you come up with alternatives."

Esther might have been surprised James had already begun researching months ago, but his team took this discovery in stride. They knew James preferred to extensively research projects before making major decisions. The fact he had already done a lot of investigation meant one major hurdle to James making a decision was out of the way. It also clearly communicated they should not waste time on researching their alternatives. James was extremely thorough and not typically open to information he overlooked unless he asked for it, like he had done in this meeting to clarify their needs.

"Obviously, time's an issue," said James. His associates continued to flip through their folders. "However, we can't afford to rush ahead with a decision only to trip up in a year's time. We must tread carefully and consider all of our options. When we go with a software solution, it needs to stick."

James went on to check if everyone could meet consistently on Tuesday afternoons to interview potential vendors and discuss their views and impressions afterwards. Once this was confirmed, James asked Travis to schedule the vendor meetings.

"Just as a point of interest," mentioned James. "While I was conducting my research, I came upon two of the largest companies that offer alternatives to our small business accounting program. One offered an on-premise solution, the other offered a cloud solution, however, I took both out of consideration because they do not make outside sales calls. They only demo their solutions online." James did not need to do any more explaining for the sake of his team. They understood James did not buy from vendors he could not meet in-person.

After the meeting, Sally and Travis were chatting as they headed back to their offices. They were both excited and thankful James was including them in on the decision for this new software.

"We won't have to worry about any more 'surprise' invoices," mused Sally.

"Yep," agreed Travis. "Plus I think James' competition with Esther will help speed things along. He must have some answers to bring back to Esther and Peter in their meeting next month."

"That's where we'll come in," said Sally, pausing in front of her office door. "Even with the preliminary research he's done, he's going to need us to help him dive deeper and share responsibility for the decision. The problem is too big for him to turn it into another 'fact finding mission' that never arrives at its destination."

Chapter 10

New to the

Game

"Interesting," said John, looking down at his paper. "Let's continue on with the next question. Does your software provide an easily accessible way to compare or review billable versus non-billable hours? And how does it differentiate between overtime, missing time and other categories?"

"That's an excellent question," replied Brent. Sharply dressed, Brent must have been one of the ERP software company's youngest reps. He sat directly across from Esther, John and the rest of the selection committee. "Yes, the types of hours, billable or non-billable, are entered by the individual. These are required fields. The type, such as overtime, is selected from a drop-down list. I'm not absolutely certain, but I believe this list is editable."

"Can the type of hours be a mandatory field?" John continued.

"I'm not certain, but I can check," responded Brent confidently.

That's the second time he's said he doesn't know the answer to a simple question, thought Esther. Her frustration was growing as she sensed this meeting was a waste of time.

"I'm curious about how your software is working for companies similar to ours. Does your software do anything unique in the way it assigns tasks or tracks progress on projects by due dates and other criteria?"

Again, as before, Brent nodded. "Our software offers very competitive functionality in those areas, but I can't think of anything we do that is totally unique."

That was it. This interview was officially over. Esther spoke up, "Alright Brent, I think that's all the questions we have for now."

"Okay," replied Brent a little taken aback by her abruptness. He paused and then added, "Thanks so much for your time."

Brent put away his laptop and closed his bag. Daryl opened the conference room door and walked him to the lobby. While they were waiting for Daryl's return, Esther looked again at the clock to see how long the interview had lasted. The meeting had started at 1:00. It was now 1:25.

Once Daryl returned, the team started to compare notes about Brent's presentation.

"Well, we've seen the tutorial he kept going on about and reviewed everything on their website, plus any online reviews we could find," said John. "Their website was helpful, but it does not give enough details. It talked so much about 'well-being' that if I didn't know better, I would've thought they were selling insurance."

"He seemed to know his stuff," piped up Jennifer, ever the optimist. "I mean, sure, he couldn't tell us all of the specifics, but at least he knew it could fix our specific problems."

"We have to look beyond his promises to the facts he provided," countered Daryl. "The problem is he did not fully answer any of our questions. How can he be sure his software will fix our problems if he can't tell us specifically how it works? I don't think he really knows much about his products."

"I prefer a rep who knows more about their product than I do," said Esther. "And I think Brent only *just* knows more about his product than us. That makes me nervous.   I don't want to be nervous about the purchase we're making. I want to be excited."

They had scheduled their first two vendor meetings back-to-back so the next meeting was in 30 minutes.   The committee agreed to return to their desks to answer phone calls or clear emails and reconvene when the next vendor arrived.

"I hope the rest of these vendor meetings go better than this one," said Esther. "If not, then we might have to go with whatever James comes up with and you know that would really fry my grits." She then crossed her eyes and the team laughed, knowing Esther would never return to James without at least one viable vendor to consider.

Chapter 11

A Gilded
Conscience

James was skeptical of Michael, the young and confident salesman, within minutes of meeting him. During the introductions Michael mentioned attending a major technical conference a few months back. When James said he also had attended, Michael smiled and boasted about how he knew many of the speakers personally.

"Dapper" was the only way James could think to describe him. The man was outfitted impeccably in a $2,000 suit and accompanying $5,000 watch. He was clearly dressed to impress. Unfortunately for Michael, this did not have the intended effect on James.

James saw overly flashy clothing or accessories as a sign of weakness. He viewed outward signs of wealth and success as an inward sign of insecurity and potentially a lack of integrity.

Michael *did* seem knowledgeable about alternatives to their small business accounting program. His software company specialized in cloud and on-premise accounting solutions for growing small-to-midsized organizations. For example, his program allowed much more flexibility when it came to billing clients. Based on agreements made with clients for types of work performed, users could submit invoices immediately following a service ticket, project phase being completed, or even on a pre-determined schedule.

However, most of his talking points focused on name-dropping the other high-profile businesses his company supposedly served in the area.

Once he left, James sat down with his team to discuss their impressions of Michael's presentation. Everyone agreed the dapper salesman was knowledgeable and his proposed solutions could be viable.

Victor and Sally thought he was entertaining, but Victor summed-up their feelings in a single statement: "The guy was slick, but I wouldn't trust him as far as I can spit."

Sally was quick to the punch, "And the last time I saw you spit, the wind blew it back onto your suit."

Everyone laughed and agreed although Michael's company may have a reasonable solution, his expensive outfit and overconfident behavior was hiding some flaws in their delivery or service process. His company needed to be on the back burner for now, but not out of the running.

The critical, fact-based evaluation of the presentation reminded James how much he loved working with this team. "So," he asked, "what do we do if every vendor who comes in here is dressed better than us?"

"That's simple," Victor chimed in, "the company has to buy us all new suits!"

James chuckled along with everyone else. "You're on. I'll buy the suits if all we get are sales vermin dressed like politicians on one condition: Before the next meeting make certain you each research the solution to be presented in more detail. I'd like everyone to have more questions specific to the solution than we did today. These meetings need to be more of a polite interrogation than a tea party."

Chapter 12

Knowledgeable

Know-how

There was something about Bob of B2B ERP that just made Esther trust him. Even if Brent had not blown his presentation due to inexperience moments before, Bob's no-nonsense yet empathetic approach gave Esther confidence in his on-premise ERP solution.

John was respectfully, methodically leading the vendor interrogation. Bob was calm, professional and knowledgeable. Before answering most questions, Bob posed one or more questions of his own to clarify their needs.

Years earlier Esther had fallen asleep standing up watching a software demo. This was a totally different experience as Bob's questions kept everyone engaged and his succinct answers kept Esther's active mine from moving too far ahead or onto other matters.

"Bob, it sounds like you guys have a great on-premise ERP solution," Esther asked as her first venture into the dialogue about 45 minutes into the meeting. "But what about the cloud? Do you have any plans to represent a cloud-based solution this year?"

"Good question," Bob replied, nodding his head. "There's a lot of publicity these days about cloud solutions. A recent survey indicated about 40 percent of respondents stated they had begun to experiment with a move to the cloud. However, the number is misleading because remember, they are <u>experimenting</u> with the cloud rather than being fully committed to it. The survey concluded cloud computing is still in its infancy.[1]

"While I can see certain applications like email being done through the cloud, we don't trust the performance or security of cloud solutions. Therefore we don't have any current plans to add cloud products to our offerings."

"I like your presentation, but I don't agree with your conclusion," Esther bluntly yet politely responded. "John, why don't you get through the rest of your list so Bob can try to convince you guys that I'm wrong?"

John smiled and continued through his long list of their needs. Bob kept impressing them as he answered every question, further explored their needs, and even helped them identify a couple of additional features for their wish list.

Everyone sincerely complimented Bob on a great presentation and thanked him for helping them better understand their needs. After Daryl returned from the compulsory lobby walk, he joined Esther and her team to discuss whether Bob's solution had merit.

Esther asked her team for their opinions. "Wow," Daryl exclaimed. "It sure makes a difference to talk with a real expert instead of a nice kid who's just starting in the business."

"Boy, that's for sure," John chimed in. "He's obviously been doing this for years. Even if we don't go with his company, he helped us better clarify our needs so we can better qualify the next three vendors."

"I don't know," Jennifer hesitated. "I'm not certain, but at times it seemed like he was promoting his solution rather than really exploring our needs." John, Daryl and Esther looked at each other. Esther was the first to smile, and then she responded.

"You're right, Jennifer," Esther said congratulating her. "I'm sure John was going to say this next, but there are certain parts of Bob's questioning and answers that are meant to direct us to his solution over any competitors, either on-premise or cloud. It's up to us to discern what parts of his presentation are incomplete or biased. He's knowledgeable and a man of integrity, but his primary responsibility is still to sell us something."

"He's definitely a front runner, but I want to talk with the other vendors," Daryl added.

"Before the next one comes in, I'll confirm some of Bob's statements by doing some research," John offered. "He made some pretty strong claims. I'll check online forums and my network to see if they agree with him."

"Okay, we have our first finalist," Esther exclaimed and she clapped. The others chuckled and joined in. "But Big Bob's biggest obstacle is no cloud. We'll have to see how your next two vendors perform, and my preferred solution from Marie."

Daryl smiled broadly and teased, "Hey, Esther, what are you going to do if we all outvote you and go with Bob's on-premise solution? Then you'd have to tell James he was right."

Esther smiled back, lifted her chin in a jokingly deferent air, and played along, "We'll see. You guys haven't heard Marie yet. The game's not over."

Chapter 13

Showing
Promise

Linda, and attractive woman in her mid-thirties, finished presenting to James and his team. She was the rep for a rapidly growing ERP software firm in the area. The company was the current darling of the tech press, which was writing glowing reviews of their cloud computing accounting solutions. However, the company was still very new and they had just a few clients.

Once Linda left Victor pointed out how professional and organized Linda was in her presentation.

James agreed, but also countered by saying Linda's company had recently won the local magazine's "Rookie of the Year" award - a title given to the most successful *new* company that had been in business for less than a year. James wanted to do business with a company that had been in business for longer than a year. He wanted tried-and true, proven solutions.

"Boss, you chose Linda's company as one of your finalists," Victor reminded James.

James shrugged and started to answer, but Travis jumped in to share a story. "Years ago the company I was working for purchased from a startup. You know, all companies are startups at one time or another. Many times I have bought from young companies and it has worked out fine. This time, that was not the case."

"What happened?" Sally asked.

"Well, everything started out well, but in this case they were undercapitalized and lacked experience in the solutions they were selling. It really turned into a nightmare. We ended-up terminating our contract with them and going with a company that had over a decade of experience in the solution. From that point on everything went smoothly.

"I don't mind working with startups," Travis continued, "but now I'm just much more thorough on the way I evaluate any company, startup or one that's been around as long as dirt."

"Well, some of Linda's executives look like they're as old as dirt," Sally added with a smile, as she pulled up their website on the computer connected to the LCD projector. Everyone laughed. "But the bottom line is Linda's company is not a group of college students. These people have decades of experience and should remain in consideration."

James nodded his head. "I agree we have to keep the experience of their executive team in mind. That's why I chose them. It may shock you, but I remember when we started out. I was very thankful for all of our early clients. The four of us had decades of experience, but it still took several years for us to learn how to work together and achieve the high level of efficiency we have today. I don't want to be part of their learning process if I can avoid it. I'm much more comfortable working with a company that has had at least three-to-five years working together so their executive team has worked out the kinks in their services."

"The problem is," Travis jumped back in, "we're talking about an ERP system that's going to run our entire company.

This is not a small, one-off application. I think it's too risky to work with a start-up on something as mission critical to our organization like ERP."

"But at least she's proposing a cloud solution for you," Victor added mockingly. "It seems Linda may have two strikes against her. Although we want to consider any viable option, I share your concerns about solutions in the cloud."

Sally chooses her words carefully before responding. "I agree they are a new company and the cloud has some potential issues, however I would like to keep Linda's company in the running for now. Although you two analyzers are uncomfortable with a cloud implementation, my sales are at risk and the cloud clearly offers us a faster, less expensive way to replace what we've got. Also, I always like to practice the Golden Rule in business. I too remember when we were a startup. I needed people to believe in us because of our former track record. I'm just asking that we keep her company in the mix for now."

James smiled and nodded approval. "That sounds reasonable to me. Now I asked you to do extensive research on each of these companies. What have you guys cooked-up to throw our next vendor victim off of their prepared script? They should be showing-up in the next 15 minutes."

Chapter 14

Misconduct

Esther ended Kyle's presentation early. Brent may have lasted as long as Kyle, but those who knew her were aware that Esther's feathers got ruffled by their latest vendor. John escorted Kyle back to the lobby from their conference room while the group smiled at each other without saying anything.

"That was... interesting," mused Daryl. "I don't think he even knew I was in the room. Esther smirks, organizing some papers on the conference table.

A few minutes later, John came back in the room. "Esther, Kyle wanted me to inform you that he hopes you have an especially great weekend. You too, Jennifer."

"Wow, thanks," said Daryl. "Esther, is it me, or was he coming on to you?"

"I definitely noticed that," replied Esther.

John slid back into his seat. "Did you notice it before you exchanged business cards with him, since your card has your cell number on it?"

"Yes. That's why he got one of my old business cards that has my disconnected cell number on it. That was an idea Dan gave me so I keep some of those around at all times. It's nice to get the compliment, but fortunately it does not happen too often."

"Ah," replied John. "Good. Well, do we want to talk about the solutions his company is offering?"

"I vote no," concluded Daryl before Esther could respond. "I have a friend at one of the companies Kyle said his firm has as a client. I texted him during the presentation to see if they like the service Kyle's company is giving them. He's their top IT guy and he's never even talked with anyone at Kyle's company."

"No," agreed Esther, shaking her head. "We need a vendor who is interested in providing an incredible solution, not someone who wants to date a married woman and is possibly a liar. He apparently has some integrity issues."

Daryl announced to the group, "Well, I don't know about you, but old Bob's software company is looking pretty good right now."

"That's because you haven't met Marie yet," Esther replied with a smile.

Chapter 15

On
Cloud Nine

"Which is why the primary method we deliver our products is through the cloud," Marie looked each member of the committee in the eye, her gaze finally coming to rest on James. "Do you have any additional questions?"

Both Victor and Sally glanced towards James, waiting for the inevitable. "Okay, so you said our administrator will need limited training because your software is so easy to use. What about the time it will take for our people to learn how to actually *use* this new application? Won't we experience decreased efficiency while we're learning how to fully utilize the program?"

Marie nodded. "There is a learning curve, but it's shorter than other competitive programs. Part of the reason your people will be comfortable with the screens is because it's designed to work with and look similar to Microsoft Word and Excel. This typically saves thousands in implementation costs."

James squinted before responding. "What if we decide to develop our own software? After all, no other company can fully understand what our company needs as well as we do. We already have some in-house IT people. Couldn't we just rely on them to develop something to get us by?"

Marie smiled. "You know the skills of your team better than I do. However we regularly replace home-grown software because over time your budget can't keep up with the billions of dollars Microsoft invests in software development. My experience is home-grown solutions are your riskiest option, in part because they also distract you from your core business   Our Microsoft Dynamics solutions can be implemented in a few months instead of the years it would take you to develop your own temporary product, and it's a fraction of the cost to develop a home-grown solution.

Victor spoke up. "Besides the development savings, why is your solution so inexpensive?"

"First, because it's Microsoft. Microsoft and its partners have a history of offering the most cost competitive solutions in the industry. The second reason is we can meet your needs from the cloud," Marie responded confidently. "Using the cloud is like paying for your electricity. You only pay for what you use as you need it. In contrast, the on-premise solutions we provide are like building and maintaining your own turbine to produce electricity for your building. There are some benefits, but the utility model of just purchasing electricity is obviously much more economical. Plus, the upfront cost is much higher for on-premise solutions."

James had heard enough. "Thank you for meeting with us on short notice, Marie. What questions did we not ask you that we should have?"

Marie paused and then replied, "I think this was an excellent first meeting. If you realize the value of investing in proven Microsoft solutions and our 20-year history as a reliable solution provider then I suggest we dive deeper into a discussion of your needs in our next meeting. I'd like to bring along Carlos, my sales engineer with me. He has implemented systems with several companies just like yours. I think he will help us more fully explore what you need today and into the future."

Travis spoke before James. "That would be great. We don't like the cloud, but we trust Microsoft and your company seems to have a good reputation. I'd be interested in comparing notes with Carlos."

"Marie," James added, "I know it's early in the process, but will you please provide three company references of your clients who are using these Microsoft solutions in the cloud? I want to see if my concerns about performance and security are correct, or overblown."

"No problem. You'll have them this afternoon," Marie promised and then the meeting ended.

Travis returned from walking Marie out to the lobby and spoke first as the group started to compare notes. "Wow, she was impressive. I know you think the cloud is going to rain on us, James, but she made some good points. And those screen shots looked like a product that could really help us."

Victor added, "We've been a Microsoft shop since the beginning. My understanding is the majority of their development budget is now focused on developing the next generation of cloud solutions. Maybe we should trust their cloud solutions too."

"Look, all I want is to close more sales," Sally said looking at James. "Marie's company has the proven track record you require, a trusted vendor in Microsoft, a lower price than an on-premise solution, and it can be implemented faster. Even if you do not want to consider a cloud solution, my vote is Marie is one of our two finalists."

"Let me reach out to my network of techno-geeks," Travis offered. "I don't believe any of them are using Microsoft Dynamics cloud solutions, but I can see if they know of anyone who is."

The conversation paused and all eyes turned to James. He waited before speaking, and then added his thoughts. "If we go to the cloud, and that is a big IF, then we will probably go with Marie's company. Linda's firm just got bumped out of consideration, at least for now. I want to do more research on Marie's company and the solutions she is recommending."

Victor couldn't stop himself. "You know if we went with a cloud solution then we'd have enough money to do that special project of yours this year instead of next."

James just smiled, got up, nodded his thanks to everyone, and walked out of the room.

Chapter 16

Specialists
Needed

"And that's why we offer both on-premise and cloud solutions. I've been in the IT business for 25 years and can say from personal experience the cloud is going to be the next major technology," stated Chris, a confident, athletically fit man in his mid-fifties.

Esther looked over some of the documents that Chris had provided. "How long has your company been in business, again?"

"About 20 years," replied Chris. "However, we only added general business ERP software during the past year. Prior to that, our company has been the number one provider of software for retailers in the area."

"What prompted the expansion?" John queried.

"Accounting or ERP software is by no means a new field for us. Our other solutions are based on accounting in retail environments. The cloud just opens-up all kinds of opportunities for us to leverage our existing skills into new markets. Companies that were living with outdated solutions due to tight budgets are now implementing new solutions that are making a faster contribution to their bottom line because they are avoiding the upfront costs of on-premise solutions.

"Based on what we've discussed, it's clear our ERP software could be a big help to you."

"Thanks for coming in," announced Esther, signaling the end of the meeting. "Daryl will see you out and we'll be in touch on next steps."

Once Daryl returned, the committee shared what they thought of Chris.

John spoke first. "I know this guy has a lot of experience working with retailers, but I don't think he's worked with our kind of company before."

Esther scrunched her face a bit and replied. "Now wait, how much different can it be to provide IT services to retailers versus implementing ERP software with us? Isn't providing ERP solutions basically an IT service?"

"It would differ a lot," replied John. "We're not a retailer selling soap or clothing. We are a project driven, professional software development firm. We have completely different ERP needs than a retailer. Our new software needs to be configured by people who have done installations for companies like ours many times before. I don't want to be some company's test case."

"It's true. They have a lot of experience. It's just not with companies like ours. My concern is they won't be able to help us understand what we don't know, or fully configure the system to meet the needs we have identified," Daryl added.

They all looked at each other. It was clear everyone agreed with John. "I see your point," said Esther. "Let's put Chris on the back burner. So... you saved Marie for last, huh? You better buckle your seatbelts folks. I think you'll be pleased with our next meeting."

Chapter 17

Rookie
At Bat

Joey was pushing valiantly and confidently through the presentation of his company's ERP solution for James and his committee.

"And so," continued Joey. "Our software will keep track of anything that's billable and collect it in a single place, making sure it has been attributed to the correct client and contract. Your invoicing process will become virtually instantaneous and fully automated."

James looked up from his brochure. "And again, I'm sorry, but did you say that your company offers both on-premise and cloud versions?"

"That's correct," replied Joey.

"And which would you recommend?"

Joey paused. "That's an excellent question. The cloud option is definitely cheaper in the short run, however many of our clients like the added control that having their equipment on-site offers them."

James waited. "That still hasn't really answered my question."

"You're right," replied Joey. He appeared to be getting flustered. "Personally, I'd go with the on-premise option, since I know the value-added control it offers."

"Great," said James. "Thanks for your time."

After Joey left, James looked to his team to comment first on Joey's presentation.

"Well," offered Victor. "He seems like a good kid. Too bad he's still in high school." Everyone smiled.

"I don't think he's ever been asked which method he prefers before," added Sally. "I'm not sure he's ever even thought about it."

"He makes me nervous," said James with a tinge of disgust. "We need software and a firm we can trust with the future of our company. Joey is a nice kid, but he does not have the experience we need and any company that would send him out to us is not someone we can trust."

James was getting frustrated. "Is there only one company in the area capable of providing what we need? I can't believe that. We have one interview left, correct?" Victor nodded in agreement.

James got up to leave the room. "We have interviewed four companies and only one is potentially viable. And it's recommending a cloud solution over an on-premises one, which is not my preference. I hope we don't have to start this process all over again after this next meeting."

Sally and Victor's shoulders visibly dropped at James' comment. "Oh-oh, here we go again..." they wondered.

Chapter 18

On Cloud Nine...

Again

Daryl could tell Esther was already eating out of the palm of Marie's hand. Marie had clearly presented the cost saving benefits of implementing a cloud over an on-premise solution. She had systematically discussed each of their needs and asked intelligent questions to explore how her solution would scale with them through additional growth. She was not missing a beat.

"That's one main thing I mentioned when we talked last year," said Marie. "If you wait too long to update your software, then your systems become overloaded. Ironically, it was your accelerated success that brought this problem to the forefront and brings us here today."

"Yes, well, I received some bad advice from a well-meaning colleague," replied Esther sheepishly.

Marie smiled. "No worries. We've all been there. Hindsight is always 20/20. Hey, at least you're growing! This is not a bad problem to have if you resolve it quickly, and that's exactly what we can do for you in our cloud solutions."

"Well," announced Esther. "I think that's all the questions we have for now. John will be in touch with you soon. Let me walk you out."

Everyone said their goodbyes. When Esther returned the committee discussed the merits of Marie's solution.

"Well, what'd you think?" Esther asked, barely containing her enthusiasm.

"I like the way her solution frees-up cash that would otherwise go towards hardware and software purchases, and IT support into activities to generate more profits," John replied.

"You're the techie, John, but I'm uncomfortable with putting blind trust in the cloud," Daryl said with concern in his voice. "Remember Bob's story of Amazon's 'Cloudgate,' where the outage of its servers put thousands of businesses out of commission for two days?"

"There is not a totally risk-free solution, including on-premise products here in our offices," countered John. "There are an increasing number of attacks on company-hosted equipment as well as those in the cloud. In the situation Bob raised, Amazon's data center was one of several that got attacked. Others that were better prepared, such as Netflix, were not as severely affected.

"The cloud is not perfect, but the fact is Microsoft will spend whatever it takes to protect their cloud business applications whereas we have a very limited budget. Their experts live and breathe security whereas I just read up on it when I have time, and my experience is limited."

Esther's mind had already moved ahead of the group. She was ecstatic Marie had gained the confidence of her team, and they might get a low-cost yet reliable solution to their problems quickly. Everyone quieted down, waiting for Esther to wrap-up the meeting.

"As you can guess, I'm pleased Marie has made a strong case, but I also don't want to overlook Daryl and Bob's concerns," Esther concluded. "Marie's company remains my top choice, but for the sake of balance I think Bob's solution should be our second finalist when I meet with James and Peter. What do you think?"

The team agreed and the meeting was over. As she left the conference room, Esther could not help but wonder... *James was having his meetings with vendors these past four weeks as well. Dan and I haven't been with James and Bridgette socially for about two months, so I wonder how his vendor interviews have gone... Could he still be <u>totally</u> anti-cloud computing?*

Chapter 19

Knowledgeable
Know-How

Bob continued with his presentation. "And this software can provide a centralized view of your company's expense trends. It will reduce processing costs, streamline expense management processes, eliminate paper receipts, and enable your employees to create and submit reports any time, from any location.

"This is especially true with a company of your size, with roughly 75 employees, where several departments are acting independently. Being able to centralize this information will be a huge boon to tracking your overall budget and following expenditures made by each department."

James paused, waiting for Bob to continue. He was trying to hide his exhilaration that Bob's company was reputable and their on-premises solution proven. When the pause lengthened, James spoke first. "Excuse me, Bob, but you are the final in a number of interviews we have conducted with several companies about alternatives to our small business accounting software and spreadsheet hell. We've heard much of this information before. To be frank, what sets your business apart?"

Bob thought for a second. "There are three reasons. (1) We are small enough to give you our undivided attention. You won't get lost at our company. Your needs will be a top priority; (2) We have technical people who are located close enough to work onsite to manage the entire implementation, or just part of it if you want to use some of your own people; and (3) We have both competitive pricing and a long history of success serving companies your size so you can trust us to deliver as promised."

"Has your company ever considered offering cloud solutions?" Victor sits back in his chair.

"Yes," replies Bob. "However, our company has a long, successful history providing incredibly reliable, high performance, on-premise solutions in offices of companies your size for over 20 years. We have researched and even tested cloud solutions for years, but we remain concerned cloud computing is not as reliable, secure, fast or less costly than our on-premise solutions.

"Especially with the recent outage of Amazon's servers and the resulting loss of service for businesses that subscribe to their service, we feel that on-premise solutions provide security and control that cloud computing cannot yet offer. Technology changes so I cannot rule out cloud computing as an option forever. We just think that today it is still too immature a platform to host your company's most valuable data."

After Bob left, James gathered his committee for discussion. "Alright people," we've talked to five providers. Give me your top two choices."

"Why two?" Travis asked.

"First, we need to narrow the list because we are under the gun to make a decision. You know how quick decisions, even when 'quick' means over a period of months, make me uncomfortable. Nevertheless I think collectively we can make a good choice," said James. "Also, I've got to have at least two possibilities for when I have coffee with Peter and Esther next week."

Both Victor and Sally started singing the praises of Marie, but even the increased savings and faster implementation timeframe offered by a cloud solution did not outweigh James' concerns about downtime and security risks. Bob had played to James' fears and he had drunk Bob's "Kool-Aid." Being the final vendor, Bob's words of Amazon's "Cloudgate" were foremost on James' mind. He listened respectfully, but was most interested to hear from Travis.

"What do you think, Travis?" James asked as Victor and Sally stopped talking. His CTO had remained quiet.

Travis looked at each of them, breathed in and stated candidly, "I don't know. Both Bob and Marie make good points and their respective positions have been validated by associates in my network. We didn't have time to discuss it before the meeting but I will tell you this, I talked to each of Marie's references and they absolutely love having their applications in the cloud.

"I agree Marie and Bob should be our two finalists, but I can't lean one way or another at the moment. I'll give you my recommendation the day before your meeting with Esther and Peter. I want to reach out to a few more people and possibly even visit some sites so I can see first-hand how other companies are using these solutions."

James nodded, but said nothing.

Victor asked, "Do you know which recommendations Esther will be bringing to the table next week?"

"Nope," replied James. "But if I know her at all, the chances of us being in complete agreement are slim to none."

Chapter 20

Cloudy
Eyes

Meanwhile across town Esther's team gathered. Daryl, Jennifer and John had worked up a detailed wish list for their finalists, a top five reasons to work with each of them, and a list of five reasons *not* to work with each of them.

Esther was excited about Marie's cloud solution. She was ready to buy, but her team was focused on making certain they nailed the details so the company was protected from a bad decision. They decided to focus their evaluation in two areas:

1. Reduce Costs

    a. Lower total cost of ownership
    b. Reduce IT hardware, software, and/or services costs
    c. Reduce data center facility costs

2. Improve Agility and Reliability

    a. Enable faster time to market
    b. Improve availability and scalability
    c. Improve disaster recovery and data backup

"Based on the facts we know so far, at this stage Marie's company comes out on top, and Bob is our second choice," John declared near the end of the meeting. Travis and Jennifer nodded their heads in agreement.

"Okay," added Esther. "That works for me. However, Travis and Victor on James' team are our insurance policy. Prepare yourselves to do whatever you have to do to complete your due diligence prior to us moving ahead. Wait until I get back from my meeting later this week with Peter and James so we have confirmed the two finalists. I hope we are near the end of this road."

Esther felt great about Marie's solution. She was convinced it blew away anything else, including Bob's on-premise option which was their second choice. Nevertheless she had a nagging feeling that she is overlooking something...

Chapter 21

Last Minute

Dancing

Travis reported back to James and the team on his two visits to Marie's client companies, and conversations with two techs at other firms using cloud solutions. "Here is what I learned:

1. "Implementations were 20-50% faster.

2. "Each firm had tracked downtime on their previous on-premise systems and current cloud applications. So far cloud downtime was less, as a matter of fact virtually zero, except for one company that got caught in Amazon's downtime. That situation was challenging, but they worked around it and continued to prefer their cloud solution. An added bonus for the tech was that he was not blamed for the downtime.

3. "Savings ranged from 20-70%, with simpler applications offering the highest savings.

4. "I talked with users as well as the IT managers, including users away from the IT managers. The users either saw no performance difference from their on-premise applications or an improvement."

Everyone paused to let Travis' report validating cloud computing solutions sink in. James avoided commenting, but moved on to report on his research. "I contacted people to validate Bob's claims of superior performance and enthusiastic clients. I interviewed four of his clients. I asked a lot of questions and they all seem very pleased with Bob's company, their service and solutions.

"There are four statements by these people that stood out to me:

"First, implementations were good, but a bit long. One client mentioned deadlines were missed, but it was because they changed the specification for the system. Another client said there seemed to always be something to upgrade or improve.

"Second, downtime was only software upgrades to the servers, although one guy had a staff person who caused downtime because he installed some equipment incorrectly.

"Third, I asked about their system scalability and in most cases they were rarely using more than 10% of the capacity of their systems for 90% of their usage.

"Last, but not least, I talked only with the IT managers and company owners. None of their employees. They agreed with Bob the cloud is too risky and preferred to have their equipment to be where they can touch it."

"James, it seems these companies are sticking with on-premise solutions because it gives them comfort rather than better performance, value or one of the other criteria we are considering," Victor questioned.

"To a certain extent you're right," James admitted, "but it's clear they are very happy with the solutions.

Victor's financial mindset was in full gear now so he was not ready to back-off. "Here's what I'm hearing you say: The implementations at Bob's clients are long and there seems to be a constant stream of system upgrades like we have today.

Downtime's not an issue unless someone makes a mistake with the equipment. They are only using a fraction of the capacity they pay for, just like us. And, in the end, it seems on-premise is an emotional decision rather than a good business decision.

"It just seems the cloud is going to be much less expensive for us, and being your controller, I have to lean towards Marie's solution. Plus, if I'm not mistaken, putting this system in the cloud means we don't need to hire that additional IT team member next year, the one that we currently have budgeted."

This launched a debate about the pros and cons of on-premise versus cloud computing. Everyone participated and it helped them finalize a comprehensive list of all their needs. They also agreed how to validate the performance claims of cloud versus on-premise solutions.

James was still against the cloud, so they decided to lean towards Bob's company with Marie's solution a solid second.

"If only Marie's company solution was not in the cloud..." lamented Victor.

James then worked on his presentation for Esther, which was one page on each preferred supplier. He thought Bob's solution should blow away anything Esther had... unless she knew Marie.

Chapter 22

Face-Off

The coffee shop get together of Peter, James and Esther started with light banter, but they each knew there were serious discussions ahead to navigate.

Esther, being the lady and most aggressive person of the group, went first. "Let's get down to business. My team interviewed five vendors. My top vendor, which we would have gone with already if I hadn't committed to meet with you both, is KQQB Group. They have a Microsoft Dynamics solution in the cloud, thank you very much James, which is awesome."

Peter was watching James for his reaction and was not disappointed. James' eyebrows jumped when Esther said KQQB Group, but other than that he did not indicate any response.

"We think the performance, security and implementation time for a cloud solution are very competitive. We like the way cloud computing restructures our internal IT infrastructure and resources on a utility model, similar to electricity. For instance, we appreciate how our people get quick access to the application without having to install and activate it on their individual computers."

"But it still takes time to implement," James objected. "Any ERP system has to be configured to our needs."

"True, but the amount of time it takes to configure a cloud solution is much less than on-premise products," Esther retorted. "And we no longer have to invest in more equipment than we use. It's more of a pay-as-you-go model like Baltimore Gas & Electric."

"Maybe, but when you do a cost analysis long-term the quantifiable cost savings are negligible," James countered. "Even though I own extra computing power for my on-premise solution, the equipment costs over time are about the same as your subscription to the cloud."

"I don't think so," Esther fired back. "You're leaving out the savings from not having staff to monitor and manage the equipment, using less power, no office space, outsourcing security to experts, and other cost savings. We also don't have to do the backups, recovery and other data protection processes. Do you realize the cost of power will exceed the cost of hardware over a three year period?"

"Okay, wait," Peter said to interrupt a conversation to nowhere. "So you have identified a cloud vendor as your first choice, the KQQB Group. What happened with your other vendors?"

"We have a second choice, and the others were too weak to consider."

"In the spirit of fair play, let's allow James to present his first choice before you reveal your next best option," Peter encouraged. Esther bowed her head and extended her arm towards James as though she was silently introducing royalty. James looked at her and smiled. Then he gracefully nodded acceptance and began his presentation.

"As you can see on this sheet, we identified a superior software product and partner to implement it with our organization," James exclaimed confidently as he passed out his one-page summary on their top choice, B2B ERP.

Again, Peter was enjoying this as though he was at the theater trying to anticipate the next scene. He caught Esther's wince at the mention of B2B ERP and smiled, but the combatants did not notice.

"Their company has been in business for decades. They have a number of clients that are similar to our company, and actually others that are similar to yours, Esther. I have personally spoken with four of their references who have lots of positive things to say about them..." At that point James was interrupted by Esther.

"Wait a minute. You didn't say the references had 'nothing but positive things to say.' You said there were a lot of positive things that were said about them. I know you too well. That means there was some negative stuff about B2B ERP or on-premise applications for companies like ours. What you leaving out?"

James frowned. "There was nothing blatantly wrong. As we know, on-premise implementations take a little bit longer. You have to manage the upgrades and security patches. There was no significant downtime except with one company because their staff guy installed some equipment incorrectly. Like both of us, they do not use much of their system's capacity the vast majority of the time. I do not view any of this as negative information because we are both aware of these attributes of on-premise solutions.

"I will say every single one of the references is very pleased with Bob's company and their ERP solutions. They all agree with him that the cloud is too risky and prefer to have their equipment where they can touch it."

Esther relaxed for a moment. She was enjoying pestering James before he knew her second choice was B2B ERP. She decided to have some fun with James by raising issues about Bob's solution. She had an edge because she used a list of questions for Bob that Daryl had given her.

"So what if you continue growing and you have more people than ever hitting your single server solution with lots of requests and it simply can't handle the increasing load?"

"That shouldn't happen because we will be monitoring the usage, but we can always add another server if it's needed," James replied.

"But then that ups your cost structure. It's not just the server. You've got the ERP application, other software, security hardware and software, and more," Esther pushed.

"True, but the ERP software can scale and that eliminates our current problem. We have outgrown our small business accounting program and spreadsheets," James said calmly. "I don't see adding additional equipment an issue."

"What if your server fails? When a server fails in the cloud it is one of a pool of thousands of interconnected servers. Because of the redundancy there is no noticeable impact to your company. In an on-premise environment it can take your entire company down," Esther challenged with a smile.

"We discussed that with Bob and are considering having multiple servers to avoid that possibility," James answered. "Look, we obviously disagree about cloud computing versus an on-premise solution. Why don't we just share our two finalists and then we can decide whether to consider each other's choices ourselves."

"Well, that's easy," Esther said with a broad smile. "Our second finalist is Bob."

James was stunned for a moment. "You dirt bag!" James exclaimed laughing. "So you just wanted to beat me up for the fun of it with all these questions?"

"As a matter of fact, yes," Esther admitted.

"Well, don't get too comfortable," James shot back with a big grin. "Our second finalist is Marie of KQQB Group."

Esther's jaw dropped as Peter started laughing. Esther shook her head and replied, "What can I say? I told you she was awesome."

"You were right," James admitted. "She is impressive and her clients raved about her company. I'm not convinced yet, but it is interesting we both have the same conclusions although we disagree who is best at the moment. How about we set aside the cloud versus on-premise arguments? Let's dive into the details of these solutions to consider how they can get as beyond our collective small business accounting software and spreadsheet hell?"

Esther agreed and Peter nodded. The next 45 minutes they compared notes and talked candidly about the positives and negatives of each solution, and the companies that would implement each technology.

"Can I make a suggestion," asked Peter. "Why don't you work together in an effort to really put Bob and Marie to the test, without telling them that you are working together? I mean pepper them with some tough questions so you can confirm their solutions really meet your requirements and their companies will provide the support you truly need. You both have certain biases that will help the other person better understand the risks of each solution."

"I'm game," said Esther without hesitation.

"Me too," added James with a nod.

"Since it appears both of these companies also have solutions for non-profits," Peter continued, "would it be okay with both of you if I sat in on Bob's presentation to Esther's team and Marie's presentation to James' team?"

"Sure," Esther and James answered together. The face-off ended with the competitors on the same side working for mutual gain. Everyone was at ease once again. The meeting ended with light conversation and sincere interest in their next meeting a few weeks away.

As James walked from the coffee shop he was struck by how Peter was joining the presentations of the second choices for her and James. He noted this was shrewd because each of them would be tougher on the person representing the technology that was not their primary choice. James wondered, *will Peter be a wall flower or join each attack with questions of his own?*

Chapter 23

Good Cop
Bad Cop

James gathered his troops in his office to prepare for war.

He actually loved professional, confrontational debates with vendors when he felt fully prepared, and that was the situation. Not only had he done his research, but his team had also. Now it was the time to apply his naturally skeptical, analytical mind to discern which of the two solutions would actually be the best for his firm today, and into the future.

James started the meeting with a smile. "Guess what companies Esther picked as her two finalists?"

"Did she know Marie?" Travis guessed.

"Yep," James confirmed. "As you might think, Marie is her first choice. Who do you think is her second choice?"

"Is it Linda, the other cloud vendor who seemed fairly capable?" Victor asked.

"No, but that's a good guess."

"It can't be Bob, because you said Esther wants to go with a cloud product," Sally concluded.

"Good guess, but you're wrong," James replied, smiling more broadly than before. "Just as Marie impressed us even though we are not crazy about the cloud, Bob was equally convincing to Esther's team. He's their second choice."

Now everyone had big smiles. James continued. "So we've decided to work together through this next stage of vendor interviews."

"I think 'interrogations' would be a more appropriate description," Sally suggested, sensing James was fully prepared to get to the facts like a determined prosecutor in a high profile court trial.

"Maybe," James admitted. "Our plan is to take nothing for granted. Our job is to interview Marie and Bob with equal fervor. We like them both. We respect them both. But we cannot trust either of them just yet. We have to fully consider what can go wrong, details they might be leaving out, and confirm specifically how their software will meet our needs today and into the future."

Travis jumped in. "We'll be chess masters. Analytical gurus who can see a dozen moves ahead so we can confirm our chosen solution can meet our needs today, and will scale with us for quite some time into the future."

"Sure, Obi-Wan Kenobi," said James jokingly as the others nodded their heads in agreement and chuckled. "Here's the approach I would like to take. Travis will be the 'good cop' in the second round of meetings and the rest of us be the 'bad cop.' Travis, will you please schedule the meetings, and put together a list of good cop/bad cop questions for each vendor at least three days prior to each discussion?"

"Sure, no problem," Travis agreed.

"Great, then our job is to review your questions and do two things," James continued. "First, confirm we agree with how you assign the questions to yourself or us; and second, submit additional questions we have for your consideration.

"Our job as a team is to be very skeptical of both solutions and do our best to make each presenter provide inconsistent answers, promise something they cannot deliver, or admit where their solution is risky. Travis, as the good cop, will ask questions that are less confrontational."

"That works for me," Travis agreed. "Are we going to focus on the feature sets of each product, key aspects of the technology, or user scenarios?"

"Good question," confirmed James. "Questions about features and functionality as they apply in actual user situations are important. Go for it. Beyond that, Esther and I split responsibility for drilling down hard on details. Our primary focus is in three areas:

"First is **performance**. We need to understand the limitations of Bob's servers, if any, and challenge Marie about access time to her cloud solution. I'd also like to know if either solution can work offline and then synch the data when you connect again.   I don't think so, but I want to confirm it.

"Second is **reliability**. Whether Esther likes it or not, awhile ago there were outages at Amazon, Microsoft, Sony and the Goggle Blogger cloud services, but we know there have been times when our servers have gone down too. We have to really understand the true reliability of a cloud solution compared to an on-premise one. And lastly...

"Third is **security**. It is risky to put our data online in the cloud, but... don't tell Esther this... but we have to be fair. All data is basically accessible when a company has an internet connection. There are a growing number of security breaches at small and large companies. Where is our greatest risk – in the cloud or on our own servers connected to the internet?"

James and his team finalized the details. Travis would schedule the meetings with Marie first, followed by Bob so they could apply what they learn from Marie to confirm B2B ERP's solution is as good as they believe it is. The meeting ended with people excited about the upcoming meetings. Resolution to their problems seemed close.

James paused before jumping onto his email after the team left his office. *Cloud computing is much more reliable and secure than I thought. This could be ugly if I have to go with Esther's solution... naw! I'll find something wrong with it.*

Chapter 24

New Best
Friends

Esther was so happy she had Jennifer take everyone's specialty coffee orders prior to their meeting as recognition for making significant progress in their quest to depart from their small business accounting software and spreadsheet hell.

"Thanks for the caffeine! I guess your meeting with James and Peter went well," Daryl remarked as he gladly received his hot java.

"Not bad," Esther replied with a wide smile she could not contain. "So who do you guys think are James' two finalist vendors?"

"Well, Marie has to be one of them or else you wouldn't be so happy," John said, popping Esther's bubble. "But I don't understand. How could James have Marie as a finalist when he hates the cloud?"

Esther was disappointed John guessed Marie so easily, but she was in much too good a mood to let that slow her enthusiasm. "Okay, so you figured it out. And Bob is their first choice." Everyone smiled.

"Since we both have the same finalists, James and I decided to work together through the next phase of interviews. Our job is to confirm just how good Bob and Marie's solutions are. James is taking a hard line approach. I suggest we take a different approach. Anyone have a suggestion?"

Jennifer spoke first, which surprised the group. "I think we should be super friendly to both Bob and Marie. People are more open about their weaknesses with friends than they are with enemies. This is also consistent with one of our company values, which is based on The Golden Rule, to treat everyone with respect."

Jennifer paused as the others considered her suggestion. Daryl spoke first. "I like the idea. I like taking an approach that is consistent with our values, but I think Jennifer identified why her way will be successful. If we do this right, it will get them talking outside of their script. They may let down their guard and be more candid about the shortcomings of their solutions."

"Sounds good to me," affirmed Esther. "Now let's talk about our key responsibilities in these interviews. I agreed with James to would focus on three areas beyond confirming the functionality of how their solutions will work for us. These are:

"First is **cost**. The expenses of an on-premise solution are front-loaded. We get most of them out of the way upfront. In contrast, the cloud solutions are low cost at first, but you keep paying. We need to really compare the total costs. Can you take the lead on this, Daryl?"

"I've already started a detailed analysis, but there are some gaps," Daryl confirmed. "I'd be happy to do it."

"The next thing is **scalability**. As we know, to scale an on-premise solution you just add more equipment, software licenses and get bigger bandwidth, but applications in the cloud scale more easily..."

"They call it elasticity in the cloud because it instantly scales as you need more computing power, bandwidth or storage," John jumped in. "I've already begun working on analyzing how much we have to worry about scalability. Remember, it's not like we have a retail site that is going to go bonkers. Our scalability requirements are minimal compared to lots of other companies. I'll take responsibility for this analysis."

"You got it," Esther agreed. "Our third responsibility is to confirm **vendor viability**. I mean, just how good are these two companies? I don't want to sign a contract with one of them and then find out later they were just good talkers."

"Not a problem," Daryl interjected. "I have already asked Jennifer to do some web searches on them, check the Better Business Bureau, and thoroughly research them with our vendor contacts. We can take primary responsibility for this too."

At that point Daryl turned to John and Esther's team began discussing questions, strategies for conversations with the vendors, and other ideas how to confirm they were making the right decision.

Esther sat silently as her team continued their discussion. This was exactly why she hired them. They dealt with the details while she drove the business forward. An unexpected thought did occur to her though. She wondered, *There's only one thing I haven't considered: What happens if James is right and the cloud makes our situation worse?*

Chapter 25

Storm
Clouds

After pleasantries James introduced Peter to Marie. "Marie, I've asked my friend Peter to join us today. I sit on the board of his non-profit organization. He may need a similar solution in the future, so he thought this might be a good use of his time."

"It's an honor to meet you, Peter!" Marie exclaimed, not missing a beat because she had researched everything about James, including his interests outside of the company. "I love the work your organization does in our community. As a matter of fact, a friend of mine is one of your volunteers. Her name is Judy Jackson. She helps out when you do events."

"Oh, I know Judy!" Peter replied with a broad smile. "She's great. Very good with people. She really helps make our events successful."

"And this is my sales engineer, Carlos, who used to work at a government contractor like your company," Marie said turning back to James. This led to introductions all around. Then Marie shifted the focus of the meeting to the questions they had sent her after their first meeting. "Travis, were you able to talk with each of the references I gave you?"

"Yes," Travis said with a smile. "Unfortunately I could not get them to say one significantly bad thing about your solution. I even went to the offices of J. Macki, plus Samson, Jonah and Park, to see your solution in action. Everyone I spoke with was pleased and the application seemed to be working well for them."

"Great," Marie then looked to James for his buy-in, but he remained stone-faced. "Then you..." Marie started, but James interrupted her mid-sentence.

"Marie, you and your solutions are very impressive, but I'm really uncomfortable with not having our systems in the back room where I can see and touch them. This enables us to resolve problems ourselves rather than wait on someone else."

Marie smiled and nodded. "I understand. There is something about having your servers, software and other equipment onsite. And in the past it was the best way to go, but times have changed and cloud computing is not a fad. Studies are showing it helps companies be more competitive and profitable.

"Remember the utility analogy we discussed. You rely on power to operate your office. Power for the coffee machine, your computers, phone system... and, let's face it, that covers the essentials because we included the coffee!" She paused and smiled for effect.

They gave her a light chuckle, and she continued. "However, even though power is absolutely critical to your business and you cannot operate without it, you don't have an electrician on staff or a backup power generator big enough to supply power to all of your electrical devices do you?" James silently shrugged his shoulders and shook his head 'no' so she could complete her thought.

"Cloud computing is the next generation of technology in part because it enables companies like yours to only purchase the computing power you need, rather than bankroll a power plant of servers and software. Owning that equipment is a cost to your operation, not an asset, because it drops in value the day it is installed. Just as you trust an outside vendor to supply power critical to your operations, we take care of your backend equipment so you have more money available to grow your business and focus on what you do best."

Marie focused on James to see if he wanted to discuss his concern more. James' eyes squinted slightly and then he encouraged her to continue. "OK, I may not be as convinced as you are about the cloud, but you make a good point. Please continue."

Marie looked around the room to confirm everyone was engaged in the conversation. "Thank you for the questions you emailed me after our initial meeting. Your first one asked me to confirm our Microsoft Dynamics solutions provide very detailed records about the direct, indirect, and overhead expenses associated with each service and product line item you bill to the government."

"Yes, but our second question was about whether your implementations comply with FAR, CAS, and DCAA requirements," Travis interrupted. "Our business is somewhat different from those reference companies. Do you have a few of our competitors that I can contact to confirm your team has the expertise to set-up our system properly? We cannot afford to be out of compliance, even for a day."

"Yes, I checked with our implementation team and identified two of your competitors in our client database," Marie confirmed confidently. "I will email you their contact information later today. Also, as you remember from our other meeting, you can manage a commercial practice from the same system as your public sector business if you ever expand into other markets."

"What about our questions on project accounting? I am concerned about how well it will perform against our needs,"

Victor asked. As the top financial officer of the company, this area was near and dear to his heart.

At this point Carlos jumped into the conversation. "I really appreciate the way you identified your bottlenecks and problem areas today, and where they may be in the future. I have good news for you. Your project managers will be able to use the Business Portal to track the financial performance of projects. This is a web-based window into financial data stored within the Microsoft Dynamics. We configure it for your organization.

"From there project managers can see the number of hours worked by each contractor, how the project compares against budget and whose timesheets are missing. This real-time data enables a project manager to determine the financial condition of any project and follow-up with customers or employees to fill gaps in the data.

"One of your competitors aggregates their data to determine job-rate structures, while their project managers review finances by accessing accounts receivable and accounts payable information through the Business Portal. The result is projects maintain their momentum because change orders have supporting data, invoices are issued almost automatically, late paying customers are identified earlier, and action can be taken to resolve the situation before the risk becomes too high."

"What about the integrated reporting between Microsoft Dynamics and its CRM solution," Sally asked, jumping back into the conversation. James was impressed at how his people kept challenging Marie. He was actually enjoying the conversation more as a spectator.

"I liked that question," Carlos replied not missing a beat and looking as confident as ever. "Our developers have built dozens of custom report generators between the accounting and CRM modules to let management easily access critical company data. Basically we automate the process of pushing financial data to the CRM database, where it is organized and separated by appropriate project accounts.

"Data from both systems are then merged to assess how projects are progressing against milestones and budget. This also helps your client relationships because you can present this information in customer reports to demonstrate consultant productivity, project execution status, and a variety of other metrics. Another key benefit is how the integration between accounting and CRM functionality enables you to refine job-rate structures so future bids for government contracts are as competitive as possible."

There was silence in the room for a moment. Marie knows from experience that she needed to let the client speak first. Victor fired his next volley, "I'm concerned about reliability. Our people can only access your solution online. What if I want to work off-line?"

"Great question," Carlos again took the lead, responding with a smile. "Actually the CRM application within our ERP suite allows you to work off-line and then the next time you connect to the internet it synchronizes the work you've done with your data in the cloud. I'm curious though, how much of your work today do you do in your small business accounting program or on spreadsheets without being connected to the internet?"

Victor thought for a moment and then responded thoughtfully. "Probably none. Obviously in our offices we have an internet connection and I can get online at home or on the road, or even in a coffee shop. Maybe requiring us to be online for your application is not such a big deal after all, particularly since every day there are more places that I can access the internet, but it's still concerns me a bit."

"What about the speed of your application?" Sally countered. "I really do not want to sit and wait for online software when our on-premise-based software is so fast. I do not have the time to wait on technology."

"Another great question," Carlos replied. "Actually the servers in Microsoft's facilities are very fast and their speed is enhanced even further through load balancing and other technologies. In addition, our ERP application is written specifically to compete with the speed of on-premise software.

"I think you'll find your testing of our application will match our results. There are no significant differences in speed between our cloud-based solution and comparable on-premise solutions. And of course, our ERP software is much faster than trying to juggle data between your small business accounting program and spreadsheets as you currently do."

"You said in our prior meeting," continued Sally undeterred, "your system can be quickly accessed by all of our people, but at what point does it slow down or max out like our small business accounting program does? I want to make certain it can scale without slowing me down."

"I understand your concern and it's a good one because a number of our competitors, even some on-premise products, start to choke at a certain number of users," Marie empathized. "We have clients with thousands of users and access speed is not an issue. Actually working over the internet forces Microsoft's developers to design the code to work smaller bytes of information than on-premise applications. Therefore you can be confident Microsoft will continue to do everything they can to make their cloud solutions competitive with the speed of on-premise products."

"One of my biggest concerns is downtime," Victor said as he jumped back into the conversation. "It wasn't long ago that Amazon and some other popular services were down for a day or more. We cannot afford to be down for hours or days because of a mistake at your company or Microsoft."

Marie and Carlos nodded in acknowledgment. Carlos turned his gaze to Travis. "Confidentially, how many hours have any of your servers been down over the past year due to equipment malfunction or other issues?"

Travis' eyes squinted slightly before responding. "I looked carefully at our downtime as part of preparing ourselves for this project. Because our servers are a bit older we have actually had two system failures over the past year that shut our systems down for a total of 34 hours."

"I appreciate your honesty," Carlos replied. "Although no one can guarantee 100% uptime, our Microsoft solutions have millions of dollars invested in failover systems and redundancy to prepare for the unexpected. There is also a guaranteed 99.9% uptime Service Level Agreement (SLA)."

James shifted gears as he joined the conversation, moving on to security. "All of our clients are government agencies and departments. The data we manage for them in our projects has to be totally secure. My concern is your cloud solution creates additional opportunities for hackers to access our clients' data. This could be catastrophic for our clients in addition to our firm."

Marie smiled slightly with closed lips and waited to make certain James was finished before responding, but Carlos jumped in. "Are you saying your data is 100% secure in your current on-premise environment?"

"No, I realize there are some risks," replied James. "But we have invested heavily to make certain the systems are as secure as possible."

"Based on our conversations thus far it seems your team is very capable. I'm sure they've done everything within their power and budget to make certain your internal data and that of your clients is secure," Marie responded. "However have you seen the news about on-premise servers of organizations much larger than yours have been hacked and had data stolen? This is happening even though those companies spend hundreds of thousands if not millions of dollars more on securing their systems than you do."

"Yes, it seems like there are a growing number of those attacks occurring. It concerns us because we might become a target because of our work for the government. It was interesting to see both U.S. and U.K. government officials recently admit publicly they view cyber-attacks as acts of war," said James.

Marie nodded in agreement and continued. "Our CTO and CFO started our company because they are paranoid about security. Their prior employer made them very uncomfortable because it allowed client data to be hosted in undisclosed cyberspace locations. Like you, they worried that if they cannot control the data, or even its whereabouts, how can they fully protect it? Times have changed. The cloud is much more secure today, particularly data on our servers at Microsoft's hosting facilities."

Carlos joined in. "Let me give you three reasons why our cloud is actually more secure than your on-premise environment.

"First, we have security technology and expertise that is superior to your own simply because our company's security budget is based on serving hundreds of clients whereas you have to pay the entire bill yourselves. Also, our expertise is combined with the billions Microsoft is investing in cloud hosting and applications.

"Travis, have you ever avoided purchasing hardware or software to better secure your servers because you did not have the budget or time to install or support it?"

"Yes," nodded Travis in agreement. "Not a week goes by without me thinking about some additional technology I would like to learn more about or implement to help further secure our server room. But we only have so much budget and our staff is always strapped for time, including me."

James' lips tightened and he scrunched his face a bit, indicating displeasure with Travis' candor. Carlos continued.

"Okay, you can be confident our cloud ERP solution is secure because we invest significantly more in security than you do simply because of our size and Microsoft partnership. Our security experience is based on hundreds of company sites instead of just one."

James interjected before he could continue. "So what you're telling me is that you guys are the security gurus and we are amateurs. So what if we don't buy into your one-size-fits-all approach to security? Although it's a tragedy for a corporation to lose data, if our servers get hacked it truly could be an act of war or something catastrophic."

"Good point," Carlos said nodding in agreement. "Your data is highly sensitive. However you can take comfort in the fact we have other clients managing government data on our cloud. It's also important to recognize we approach every client implementation as a unique solution. We may leverage our experience, but we do not think clients are best served by a one-size-fits-all solution. Also, not all clouds are the same. For instance, the security system we have designed for our ERP solutions is significantly more comprehensive than a social networking site.

"This actually brings up my second point. Our security is configurable based on your needs. We develop a custom strategy for moving your data onto our cloud that offers the maximum possible protection. The number of security layers may vary based on the application within our ERP solution that you're using, however it is totally under your control.

"My third point is simple. Microsoft's hosting facilities are SAS70 certified. There is no higher security standard for general business applications. Individual small organizations your size cannot afford to meet these stringent requirements with their on-premise systems."

Carlos then went on to explain specific aspects of security built into their ERP solution. Although James, Victor and Sally tried to punch holes in his explanations, they were unable to identify a flaw. Furthermore Travis asked a number of questions to clarify his statements and each time Marie's ERP solution came out looking even better. Even James was impressed.

After Marie and Carlos departed the team compared their conclusions. Everyone admitted that although the Microsoft Dynamic solution was solid, the main reason to work with Marie's company was their expertise in implementing the Microsoft cloud-based solutions at companies similar to theirs. She and Carlos had overcome every one of their primary concerns.

Travis looked at James and said apologetically, "Sorry. Although no solution is perfect, it appears Microsoft is betting billions on the cloud and Marie's team really knows how to implement a high-performance, reliable and very secure cloud solution. Your guy, Bob, is in for quite a battle."

James nodded in agreement and shrugged his shoulders. "Thanks everybody. You guys were awesome today. The ball's in Bob's court now."

Chapter 26

Surprise

"Hi, Bob! It's great to have you back," Esther said enthusiastically. "We have lots of questions. As you know, you are one of our two finalists."

"Thank you, it's an honor to be here," Bob replied sincerely. "You're clearly a great company and it would be an honor to work together."

"A friend of ours, Peter, is also joining us," Esther said, introducing Peter. "He may just listen, but we've encouraged him to ask any questions he wants."

"No problem. Glad to have you join us Peter," Bob said with a smile and a nod. "Where do you work?"

"I'm the executive director at a non-profit in the area," Peter replied. "Esther sits on our board of directors. Thanks for letting me listen in. At some point we may need to be considering a solution so I thought this might accelerate my learning curve." Before Bob could reply, John started with his questions.

"One of the things that attracted us to our small business accounting program was its strong user community and the large number of add-on products from independent software vendors," John began. "It appears your solution has a good user community, but the number of add-on products is limited compared to our current program. What experience does your company have with add-on products to your core ERP solution?"

"There can be thousands of add-on products or just a few, but it still comes down to the expertise of your technology partner. Our role is competently implementing and supporting a limited number of add-on products that specifically apply to the primary types of businesses we serve," Bob replied comfortably. "Although we have fewer third party applications available, some are written specifically for software development companies like yours."

"Your website says you have over 200 clients," John continued. "How many are software developers?"

"Our primary client markets are government contractors, software developers, non-profits, and companies with general accounting needs that need to upgrade from small business accounting software to a true ERP solution.

"We have 23 software developers as current clients and another 57 I was able to identify had purchased from us, but the companies were sold, merged or closed," Bob responded, having anticipated this question and done his homework.

"Thank you for your proposal," Daryl said, joining the conversation. "I have some questions. First of all, you quoted the software licensed two ways: As a license fee per user and by purchasing modules. What is the advantage of one over the other?"

"The licensing by user model requires each person to have a license to access the module or modules of that license. The pricing by module requires you to purchase each module individually, but then there are a limited number of users with access privileges per module.

"If you only need limited functionally then purchasing by module typically saves you money. The trade-off is module pricing limits your ability to scale your ERP system. For most companies, purchasing individual user licenses is a better value and a wiser investment because you can have larger numbers of people on the system who are using more of its capabilities."

"So you are trying to help us not pay for full system access for the people in the company who do not need it," Daryl observed.

"Yes," replied Bob. "We realize this is an investment for you and part of my job is to help you achieve the highest possible ROI. The 'named light licenses' limit access to viewing data and running reports. They can always be upgraded to full user licenses in the future if your needs change."

"Our human resource software charges based on the number of the people we are tracking in the system, rather than the people who are accessing the system. You are only charging for concurrent users rather than anyone who has access to the system. Why is that?" Daryl continued.

"You have consultants, project managers, and engineers who need to enter billable time. Your accounting people need full access. Your sales people need to manage their pipeline, record client conversations, and drive their sales process. Marketing folks are managing their campaigns. Esther wants her reports, yet will be entering some data herself. Unlike your HR system where employee interactions with the system are occasional, our ERP solution is used by most of your people daily to be more productive in their jobs," Bob answered.

"Charging by concurrent users means you can have a certain number of people on the system at a time. Often you have less than half of your people working with the application simultaneously. It is less expensive to purchase concurrent licenses than regular ones, but you can go with just regular licenses if you prefer. Sometimes concurrent licensing can be frustrating when people cannot get on the system."

"That would drive me nuts," Esther said with a frown. "Please quote us both ways, concurrent and regular licenses. We have people who can't access our small business accounting system now and I don't want to deal with that problem again.

"Actually, he already provided us with those numbers," Daryl said before Bob could respond. "Bob gave us a number of options, including full information on the price differences between concurrent and regular licenses. We can go through it later."

"Bob, are upgrades covered in your maintenance agreement?" Daryl asked, switching topics.

"During the three, five or seven year term of our agreement, your maintenance covers tech support, maintaining the licensed version of your software, and all new releases," Bob explained. "We also make certain you have the minor upgrades, bug patches, and other fixes you need for your system during the term of our agreement. We have included only the modules you need today and in the near future. This not only lowers your initial investment amount, but your annual maintenance fees. If you need to add more modules or upgrade the system in the future, it is easy to do.

"Is any training included in your maintenance fees?" Daryl added.

"No. Training is separate," Bob responded. "I did include some training in the proposal. This is all I expect you to need initially."

"The maintenance fee is a lot," Daryl lamented. "Is it really worth it?"

"All of our clients have maintenance contracts," Bob replied assuredly. "It may seem when you are first purchasing the solution or after a major update is released that you could save some money by letting the maintenance expire. The problem is then you lose tech support, access to patches and updates, including those for payroll and tax changes, you miss out on promotions, and the major releases. Maintenance is like insurance. None of us like paying for it, but it is a wise investment."

"My last question is, are there any hidden costs to your solution versus a cloud product," Daryl asked with a sincere smile.

Bob smiled back before responding. "I think you are very familiar with the costs of an on-premise solution because you have those assets today. Therefore the solution we proposed for you should have everything you need.

"I do not have direct experience with cloud solutions. I can only report what I have read and heard from prospective clients, like yourselves, about their thoughts and experiences with cloud computing. I am not in the camp of people who believe you should avoid the cloud because the U.S. government can access your data. I do not believe some of the other lunatic fringe, conspiracy theory stuff about the cloud either.

"We have been in this industry for a long time. Cloud computing is a dream come true for the vendors. It moves people away from owning their software and using it indefinitely to having to pay a monthly subscription for it, or the application can be turned off. All of the larger software vendors have wanted this for decades, but the computing power to support it was not available. Now the internet, faster processors, quicker hard drives, and other technology make it feasible.

"We believe cloud computing is here to stay, but it will not eliminate on-premise solutions. There will be both, and each will continue to evolve and improve. The hidden cost of cloud computing is simply that you do not own it. You rent it and therefore there is never a way to turn off the cost without losing access to your solution. This is one reason many companies are doing some smaller applications like email in the cloud, but keeping their core business software in-house on their own servers."

"Bob, one of our problems is scalability," John began. "I know on-premise environments well and am not concerned about our ability to scale with your solution. But in all fairness, I am curious about your thoughts on the elasticity of cloud computing solutions as they compare to yours."

"Good question," Bob responded. "The cloud folks like to talk about elasticity by using a car's transmission as an example. Just as a car's transmission smoothly adapts the speed of the car's wheels to the engine speed as you apply more pressure to the accelerator, your cloud applications expand and contract according to demand. The key difference is you have capacity as demand increases and then it is released when it is not needed.

"As you know, with on-premise, you have all the scalability you need. I think it's important to remind ourselves your applications and your company do not have serious scalability issues from a hardware perspective. The software we are recommending easily scales for your needs as you hire more people. It's not like your current small business accounting program. You can have thousands of people accessing our software without any noticeable delay in access speeds.

"The bottom line is scalability is not an issue with our solution. The cloud's elasticity is important for companies like retailers or others with websites that may attract huge spikes in the number of people visiting or transacting on their websites. This is not the situation for companies with 50-100 employees like yours."

"That was my conclusion also," John affirmed. "Is there any situation you can see where scalability might be an issue for us?"

"At some point you may grow so large that you need more hardware to expand the capabilities of your system," replied Bob. "Certainly either in the cloud or our solution you have to purchase additional licenses for new employees, but that's not really the scalability issue you're asking about. The core software we are selling can support organizations with 10,000 or more employees. You'll never have the slow access issues you've got on your current small business accounting program again."

"I have enough trouble with the 50-plus people I have today. I can't imagine having to deal with 10,000 people," Esther lamented. "At that point I'll let John and Daryl run the company."

There was a pause in the conversation. Bob decided to break his rules of negotiation and speak first. "John, you've been around a long time and have developed software on a variety of platforms. It seems my primary competition is a cloud-based solution. I have shared our concerns about the cloud. As an expert with on-premise systems for more than a decade, do you believe a cloud solution can be as secure, reliable and perform as well as an on-premise product?"

John smiled, and did something unexpected that concerned Bob. John shrugged his shoulders. Then he replied, "You know, if you had asked me that question before we started this whole process I would've immediately agreed with you that having our own servers on-site is the best solution. However based on the research I've done and the conversations we've had with all of the vendors we considered, I'm not so convinced today."

This time Bob followed his rules of negotiation and remained quiet. John continued. "I do not think reliability and performance are the issue because in general both platforms, cloud applications and those residing within on-premise servers, are reliable and are going to perform well based on our experience, research, and actual users we've contacted.

"My main concern is security and my conclusion may surprise you. It's becoming clear that for a variety of reasons tens of thousands of small business servers are being attacked to steal data or to take control of websites to run scams or infect other computers. I wish I had a more recent statistic, but between early 2008 and mid-2009 the number of cyber-attacks blocked by IBM's X-Force security division jumped from less than 10,000 to over 500,000 attacks a month.[2] I'm sure this number is much higher today.

"Our company is not an expert at internet security and we do not want to become one. These attacks can be extremely difficult to detect and remove. Plus, if our servers became infected, our systems will be blocked and inaccessible for possibly weeks. It would be a real pain.

"I just don't know that we want to invest the time and money to try to secure your solution as competently as for instance, Microsoft will be protecting their applications in the cloud. Their best-of-breed data centers combine the latest technology, firewalls, and the highest possible levels of redundancy to give us multiple layers of defense we can't afford to do on our own."

"As you know, there have been a number of attacks on large hosting companies," Bob countered firmly, but politely. He was cut short by John.

"Yes, you walked us through those situations before. Let me be clear: I'm not against your solution or your company. All the research we've done indicates your application will do the job for us and scale with our organization as we continue to grow. Your company can provide services as an outsourced IT department for our organization. I'm confident you would do a great job. That being said, clearly Esther is leaning towards a cloud solution. We have to line up the positives and negatives of each solution and the company providing it, and then make our decision."

There was silence in the room. Bob knew he was about to lose the opportunity, so he played his desperation card. "Thank you for your candor. My expectation was that you would talk with people who have had difficulty with cloud applications. Since that has not happened, would you like to speak with two of our clients who had bad experiences in the cloud and decided to go back to on-premise systems?"

"Well, why didn't you bring those clients up before?" Esther asked with some irritation in her voice.

"I don't like to sell by bringing up negative information if I can avoid it," replied Bob. "In this situation, your research on our company and solution indicates we are great fit for your organization however you are still leaning strongly towards the cloud. I'm okay if that's the decision you end up making, but it does seem your research is missing the perspective of people who have had the cloud fail them. I am just offering to help you complete your research."

"I'd be happy to give them a call," John answered before Esther could reply. "Please send me their contact information and I'll reach out to them immediately."

After John walked Bob out to the lobby and returned, Daryl opened the conversation about the meeting. "Well, that strategy of being Bob's new best friend didn't seem to work out that well. Did we learn anything new except that he has two clients that used to be in the cloud and John may be willing to support a cloud solution in our company?"

Everyone looked at Esther. "Actually I think it went quite well. We had a candid, friendly discussion. Bob was as professional as ever, but brought up the two clients that had bad experiences in the cloud as a last-ditch effort to win our business. His timing makes the information look bad. He should have offered an opportunity to talk with these companies earlier in the process."

"They appear to be a good company and their solution certainly would meet our needs," John offered.

"My concern is the cost," Daryl said.

"My concern is the time to implement. We need a solution a year ago," Esther added.

They discussed Bob's solution and company for about fifteen more minutes. It was clear Bob was very impressive, his solution would meet their needs, and his people should be very capable. The only negatives were a longer implementation timeframe and higher costs, which were significant drawbacks. They ended the meeting with John committing to interviewing the two clients of Bob's that had negative experiences with the cloud and report back.

As she headed back to her office, Esther was pleased the team was leaning towards a cloud solution provided by Marie's company, but she had one concern. *What if Bob's ex-cloud folks brought up issues with the cloud they had not considered? That might make things very confusing.*

Chapter 27

Second
Wave

James team went equally hard on Bob, even though they preferred his solution, because of the friendly competition with Esther's team. They did not want her team to identify something they overlooked.

Bob knew he was in a stronger position with James' team. He also had considered what he did best with Esther's team and where he could improve. One change he made was to forward the contact information for the two clients that had bad experiences in the cloud to Travis before arriving at James' offices.

After Bob left the team silently looked at James, who asked them, "Well, what do you think?"

"I suspect you know what we think," replied Travis. "Let me give you one piece of information that was not part of the meeting. Bob emailed me this morning contact information for two companies that had bad experiences with cloud computing. Fortunately I talked with each of them before joining this meeting.

"Please understand I was rather tough on these references because I don't want someone who is Bob's buddy telling me the good, but not the bad about Bob's company or their solutions. It turns out one client got caught in Amazon's shutdown and it scared them off the cloud. That's like us having a server crash and moving to different technology. Other than that crash, the client admitted they loved the cloud for the same reasons it tempts us. I don't think the cloud was the issue for the other client, but rather they chose the wrong technology. They hired Bob's company to replace their cloud solution."

James paused before responding as he processed this new information. "So, Bob tried to shoot down the cloud with two of his clients that have moved back to on-premise systems, but you feel their reasons for buying his solutions do not negatively reflect on the cloud. Am I correct?"

"Yes. I am not saying cloud solutions are without problems," Travis went on. "I'm only saying each platform has its positives and negatives. Bob's two horror story clients turned out to be kids' fables instead. The risks are real in any solution we implement."

James nodded. "I still have some concerns about the cloud, even though those references did not pan out. I favor Bob's company and solution, but this has to be a unanimous team decision."

Victor challenged James' conclusion. "But can we live with the longer implementation time and higher costs? Our profits have been hit lately because of the problems our software is causing. Travis, what changed with the company Marie referred us to that is also a government contractor when they went with her solution?"

Travis replied, "Like our company, their government contracts require them to comply with the strict job-costing and timesheet management regulations of the Federal Acquisition Regulations, with supervision from the Defense Contract Audit Agency (DCAA). They also needed a reliable system to aggregate information, robust reporting, and project-accounting, which would enable the company to generate responsive project bids that were more competitive.

"They were using a small business accounting program to manage timesheets and account for projects. The company spent two weeks at the end of every month aggregating paper timesheets, keying the data into spreadsheets, and feeding it into their accounting program. My understanding is we are spending about the same time trying to manage our spreadsheets into our system.

"The DCAA actually contacted them to do an audit when they were still running their small business accounting program and they barely passed. At that point they realized the necessity to take immediate action to move beyond their accounting software and spreadsheet hell. They needed a simple way to calculate labor, fringe, overhead, and other indirect costs required to determine real-time project profits, and track timesheet status and approvals.

"In their case, they were already using Microsoft Dynamics® CRM for pursuit management and Microsoft Office SharePoint® Server to share company documents. They wanted a new project-accounting solution that would integrate with existing systems so they wouldn't have to re-key in data and to provide customers and management with detailed reports.

"They researched traditional project-accounting solutions, but found the cost of implementation too high. The company also checked with Marie, whose company had implemented their CRM and SharePoint solutions. Her team gave them a detailed project plan to set up, implement, and train employees on the system. The deployment took just six weeks."

"That sounds great," exclaimed Sally.

"So do you have the specific benefits they achieved from the new system?" James asked.

"Yes," Travis replied. "It's impressive, particularly considering they were facing similar problems to our own. The system has enabled them to integrate their new accounting solution with existing systems, create customer reports, and become compliant with their government-mandated Cost Accounting Standards. In a little over one year since the deployment, they have grown 50% in revenue, nearly doubled their employee count, decreased auditing time by 50 percent, and reduced book-closing time by one week."

"Can you give me more detail?" James asked, still struggling not to be impressed by the quick deployment time for their cloud solution and the significant benefits. He could not help but wonder how much faster his company could be growing if their accounting problems went away.

"No problem. Let me break it down into four areas," Travis assured him, focusing on the report on his laptop.

"First, they are **Exceeding Client Expectations**: They now provide clients with timely and accurate reports containing all the pertinent information about project milestones and prices. Clients are informed about project progress and how their money is being spent. Trust in their company is way up along with customer satisfaction and sales, because projects are consistently being delivered on time and within budget.

"Second, their **Existing Systems Were Leveraged**: They extended the capabilities of Microsoft Dynamics and the Business Portal module by connecting them with their existing Microsoft Dynamics CRM and Office SharePoint Server solution. This also retained the look-and-feel of their systems so they remained easy for their people to use and they could apply more features of the system to help their business."

"But we don't have Microsoft CRM or SharePoint," Sally challenged. "Will we be able to get as much from Marie's solution without having that first? And, will it be that easy for us to use?"

"Yes, it will," Travis replied patiently. "We do use Microsoft Office and the Dynamics product line builds upon that interface. Let me share the final two major benefits they feel they are receiving.

"Third, is **Accelerated Accounting Processes**: This is a big one for us. They totally automated their timesheet processes. Once contractors and employees submit their timesheets, they can close the books in three days, eliminating the need to manage paper timesheets or tons of spreadsheets.

"The automated processes with real-time updates enable accountants to analyze and report data quicker, and with more accuracy. The result is people working on a project can review and analyze project costs in real time. They have immediate access to project profitability, funding utilization, and performance against budget, without waiting for finance to finish their reporting."

"I'm okay with that," Victor chimed in. "Less calls from project teams means we can focus on other work. Have they been audited again since this change?"

"Yes, they have," Travis confirmed. "Their data is now so well organized that they actually gave the auditors access to the system. They didn't have to gather additional documentation or answer any questions. The audit found nothing in their processes, accounting policies, or even in any of their internal controls that was problematic. This is why they have decreased auditing time by 50 percent."

"Boy, would I love to see that happen," Victor commented hopefully.

"You can," said Travis. "Here's the fourth benefit they felt was significant."

"They are experiencing **Faster Company Growth**: They have grown 50% in about one year since deployment and have nearly doubled the number of their employees. However, they have only had to hire one additional member to the accounting team to accommodate the growth.

"Wow," Sally exclaimed. "I bet this could help qualify us to win substantially more contracts. We would be able to bid much more efficiently and profitably with our government accounts."

"Yes, but we should be able to do that with any new solution," James countered, not willing to give up on an on-premise product. "Bob's solution is solid and offers similar benefits.

Sally was getting frustrated, in part because her compensation depends on happy customers and sales growth. She decided to improvise and throw out an idea. "I have a suggestion. Instead of considering cloud or on-premise, isn't there a hybrid approach we could try that uses both? Marie mentioned her company provides both on-premise and cloud solutions. Why not implement our accounting as on-premise and our CRM needs in the cloud? Then if we want to go totally to the cloud or back to on-premise in the future it will be easy to do?"

Travis added, "That might give us the best of both worlds, James. We know you are impressed with Marie's solution, but you just have a bias towards walking into the server room to see your systems. It makes you feel more secure, but after these presentations I think it's clear the data on the equipment back in our server room is not any safer than in the cloud. If we have an internet connection, hackers could get to our data, and probably a lot easier than if our data was protected in one of Microsoft's multi-billion dollar secure hosting facilities."

A polite debate ran for thirty minutes as James fought for physical presence, Victor argued costs, Travis provided reasons for and against both solutions, and Sally pushed hard for a fast solution.

In the end James could sense he was outvoted. At the very least, part of their new solution was going to be in the cloud. It might even all go there because his Scottish bloodline hated wasting money, which the on-premise implementation seemed to do.

Victor broke the silence, knowing he had to force James' analytical nature to agree to a timeframe to choose. "James, the decision is ultimately yours. When are you willing to commit to make your decision?"

James looked around the room and smiled slightly. He really appreciated how committed his people were to his company. They were really taking ownership for this decision. He breathed in deeply and then replied.

"Today is Tuesday. Travis, you have two days to talk with any additional references from Marie and Bob, if they have them, of clients who have implemented a hybrid solution. Get back to me with their experience by Thursday evening." Then looking at the team he added, "You'll have my answer after my meeting with Esther and Peter on Monday."

Chapter 28

Love Fest

Esther's team loved Marie, but Daryl and John hit her hard with questions because they did not want James' team to find something they overlooked. Esther was a bit surprised, but relaxed and appreciated how her team was confirming key details she had not considered. Esther was also comfortable because Marie had an answer to every challenge... until Daryl surprised the group with a new idea.

"Marie, I think you know we are leaning in your direction, subject to your pricing and other details. Of course, my primary concern is pricing," Daryl continued. "However my second issue is what if we make a mistake? We have to know our options. So I have one challenge for you. If you can pass this test, then you may have a sale." He paused for effect, and then continued.

"What if we go with your cloud solution and are unhappy with the results for any reason? Can we move our data to an on-premise solution and get a credit from your company and/or Microsoft because the cloud did not live up to its hype?"

"I'm not aware of that type of guarantee," Marie responded smiling. "Certainly we could consider some kind of credit on the work we have done, or at least it will be much faster to implement the same project a second time. I'm not sure how much could be ported from a cloud solution to servers in your offices, but as you know, we do supply both types of systems. I'll check with my people and Microsoft to see what we can do. Then I'll get back to you, hopefully by Friday."

"If you protect our jump to the cloud, Marie, and your pricing is competitive, then I guarantee you have our business," Esther exclaimed. Then realizing she could not speak for the team, she quickly backtracked a bit by adding, "Of course, if the team likes your guarantee and pricing. They don't let me make big decisions on my own."

Everyone laughed, including Esther. They understood her and appreciated her commitment to be held accountable by the group. They wrapped-up the meeting and Esther walked Marie to the lobby.

When Esther returned to the conference room, the team compared their conclusions. Daryl spoke first. "I vote for Marie's solution. It's the least expensive and it will positively impact our business faster than Bob's. It's not that Bob's solution is bad. I just think we need to save the money and move more quickly."

Esther looked at John expecting him to have a strong opinion, but Jennifer jumped in first. "I know I'm the most unqualified person in the group to have an opinion, but I agree with Daryl. His reasons are good, but I've also thought a lot since we started this process about how often I am doing work for this company without an internet connection. I mean, that's a big argument against the cloud. The only times I could think of being without the internet were when I was on a hiking vacation and on airplanes. Big deal! I shouldn't be working on vacation and other passengers might see my stuff if I work on an airplane, so I think our people will be just as productive using a cloud solution."

John smiled and added his thoughts. "The major airlines are adding internet access to all of their flights. So I guess your only remaining escape from the online world is your remote hiking vacations, although I do know some hikers who get great reception on their cell phones. Maybe soon there will be nowhere for you to hide." They all chuckled and then John began to share his thoughts.

"Although our homework for James was to focus on cost, scalability and vendor viability, I think the cost and scalability issues are pretty straightforward when you consider our needs. We can compare them fairly easily. My concerns fall into three areas: Security, validity, and vendor viability. Let me walk you through each of my conclusions to see if you agree.

"Our research concludes our data is never totally safe even if it's on servers in the other room. Either way we implement, we have to decide the level of security to have in the system. Current encryption technologies like keys and communication methods such as secure socket layer and 'tunneling' techniques like a virtual private network provide great protection when supported by sound business processes and good employee discipline."

"What's the socket thing and virtual network you're talking about?" Jennifer asked.

"Sorry. I was trying to make it easier for you to understand by giving you the full name of the technology instead of its acronym. Secure Socket Layer is often referred to as 'SSL,' and a Virtual Private Network is a 'VPN.' It's probably not worth going into detail about it," John explained patiently.

"I agree. Keep going," Esther urged.

"The bottom line is top notch security on our own servers is going to be expensive, need constant monitoring, and have to be updated often as security technology evolves. I don't know that we want to go to this expense and the risk of managing it. Another option is to outsource the management of the system to Bob's company. There are other risks in going with

Microsoft's cloud, but I'd rather they invest their billions in protecting our data than we do it on our own."

"Okay, what about your second concern?" Esther prodded.

"Next is validity," John continued. "If we're going to the cloud, we have to validate how we are going to use the application just as rigidly as we would an on-premise solution. We have to make certain we have all the details on where our application is hosted, the technology operating it, the security protecting it, how well it meets specific needs we have, and how it helps us meet the regulatory requirements we have to meet. We have to be to be more than comfortable with these details. We have to be totally confident Marie's solution fully meets all of our requirements. I think we are close to thoroughly validating her solution and Bob's. Do you all agree?" They did.

"My third concern is vendor viability. We have interrogated Marie, talked with her references, done web searches on her company, thoroughly investigated the Microsoft Dynamics solutions she is recommending, researched the viability of these solutions in the cloud, and done everything we can to confirm Marie's company and this solution will meet our needs today and into the future. We have also done the same with Bob's solution."

"So what about Marie's references?" Daryl asked. "What were the key benefits that relate to our company?"

"Her references were very helpful. I even got online with some of them to view their screens," John replied. "Here is a summary of how their businesses improved, from my point of view.

"The first benefit involves **Data Migration**. It was not high on our list, but in retrospect it should have been. How do we move our existing accounting data to the new solution so we have past data to help our decision making?

"One of their clients migrated 10 years' worth of transactional data from their small business accounting program to Microsoft Dynamics so their accounting staff could use historical data in their analysis and cost estimates. It took a week, which is great when you consider mapping our existing accounting software's fields into a new Microsoft Dynamics chart of accounts. They didn't lose any historical data during the process.

"Also, we don't have to instantly stop using spreadsheets. The integration between Microsoft Dynamics and Microsoft Office allows our people the ability to quickly import and export data to edit and update financial information, which simplifies the auditing process."

"I was wondering how we were going to live without any spreadsheets at all," Daryl commented.

"No worries," John continued.

"Next is what I call, **Tools and Tricks**: "Remember how we liked the large library of third party applications for our current accounting software. Well, the Microsoft Dynamics third party library has some great options too. For example, we can use ImageLink to attach images or scans to every transaction or purchase order, and FIDO from Sandler Kahne to enable our accounting team to isolate and compare data points in the general ledger for reports.

"Also, Marie's team created personal views in Microsoft Dynamics for each department so the user interface would retain the look of familiar programs. For example, they customized a 'project net profit' screen so project managers can drill down into each engagement to view costs by line item, pull up supporting documentation with ImageLink, and create status reports. Project managers can also use this screen to analyze a standard budget versus an actual report. She showed it to me in an online meeting. It was cool.

"Then there is, **Tracking Project Profitability**. This involves our challenges tracking time and expenses entered by our people and contractors. One client had similar problems to ours.

"Their company tracked project activities and accounting data across spreadsheets and their small business accounting program so it was practically impossible to compare current project cost information against estimates. The project managers updated project information in spreadsheets, including material and labor costs. The accounting staff would then have to re-enter this data into the company's accounting system to generate accounts payable records. It typically took them a month to understand the full costs of any given project. With their new Microsoft system, the data was ready in real time without any re-entry."

"At least we're not that bad," interjected Daryl. "We're typically only a week or two behind."

"True," agreed Esther, "but remember that big project last month. It took almost four weeks to get it right, and although we're often at 1-2 weeks, that is still too risky. We need this information real-time for our sake and to protect our clients. The other problem is, as we have grown it has become more difficult to track comparable projects managed across the regions we serve or efficiently allocate resources geographically."

Daryl nodded in agreement as John started again.

"Tracking comparable projects and resources was a problem of theirs too. The work this company does requires four levels of accounting detail, plus a description confirming

111

work that was performed. The four levels are the project number, the jobsite, the equipment involved, and activities performed. Most accounting packages only allow for two levels, but Microsoft Dynamics allows you to configure additional levels of accounting detail without paying for costly customizations.

"Using the Microsoft Business Portal for internet access, employees and contractors enter time and requests from anywhere, but that's not all. Depending on the approval workflow we define, our clients and/or internal managers can approve or reject requests from any internet connection because they can see the real-time data in their browser.

"This creates two significant benefits: First, their accounting personnel now work online instead of on paper or a variety of spreadsheets; and second, daily time reporting and project profitability is available as soon as the data is entered."

"Do you have any more detail on the benefits? Like maybe something I would understand," Jennifer asked.

"Aw, c'mon!" John encouraged with a smile. "You've been tracking with me each step of the way. But, as a matter of fact, I do have a short list that may interest you and conclude my report on Marie's references. Here they are:

"First, invoicing used to be a problem. Now over 90 percent of their invoices are out by the fifth day of the following month.

"Second, saving 20 days on issuing invoices means their clients are receiving their bills about three weeks earlier and paying much sooner.

"Third, client satisfaction is up and invoice disputes down in part due to the four levels of accounting detail, plus a description on every invoice, and clients receive them sooner so they remember the work better.

"Fourth, audits and client requests for additional data are a breeze because now they can respond within minutes instead of the hours it previously took to gather the information by hand.

"Fifth, profitability is up because projects are now tracked real-time so adjustments can be made before costly problems destroy the opportunity.

"Lastly, the sixth benefit is the company has grown significantly, but their accounting department is supporting the growth with one less person."

"It sounds like a dream for me," Daryl commented with a wide smile.

"So you vote for Marie's solution, subject to Daryl approving the pricing?" Esther asked John.

"Yeah, I'm okay with it," John said. "I certainly have too much to do already. I don't want to manage this system if I can avoid it."

Esther wrapped-up the meeting. "Okay, well it sounds like we agree Marie's solution is the best for us. Daryl, please get final quotes from Marie and Bob. If you get those to me on Thursday then I'll give you my final answer after my meeting with James and Peter on Monday. Thank you all for your hard work on this project, but keep in mind, the decision is the easy part of this process. Then we have to work with the winning company to implement."

Esther purposefully avoided mentioning Marie's promise to check with her company and Microsoft about moving their data if the cloud turned out to be less than they hoped for. She wondered, *Has Daryl had set an expectation that could not be met?*

Chapter 29

Combined
Forces

Esther met with James and Peter after the non-profit's board meeting. She was looking forward to comparing notes and moving on with implementing a solution.

"I suggest before you share your final decisions, the two of you first explain your findings. You can then debate your way to the solution you feel is best for each of your companies," Peter proposed.

"That sounds fine with me, but what happened to you, Mr. Wall Flower?" I thought you would ask Bob at least one question," Esther declared.

"Me too," James chimed in. "You just sat back and observed with Marie. At least you didn't fall asleep."

Peter smiled and paused before answering. "It was actually refreshing to be part of two meetings where I did not have to say anything. I'm always facilitating, leading, or participating. All of that requires me to talk. I really enjoyed observing your people, studying the sales styles of Bob and Marie, and learning about their solutions."

"So did you make a decision about what you should do?" Esther asked.

"Let's focus on the work the two of you have done. I'm not the priority here," Peter replied. Esther and James agreed.

"My team interviewed Marie and Bob as we discussed," Esther began. "We were asked to focus on three areas: Cost, scalability and vendor viability.

"First, let's talk about **cost**. Bob's on-premise solution involves purchasing hardware and software, providing air conditioned space to house it, and then having people to manage, monitor, update and be available 24/7 if the server goes down to bring it back up again.

"We do not want to manage the equipment, so we would outsource that to Bob's folks. It is an expense, but less than us doing it in-house.

"The upfront cost compared to the cloud is steep, but consistent with what we expected. Our big problem is the tax code. Why should we depreciate Bob's solution over a number of years when 100% of Marie's cloud solution is a write-off the year we pay for it? We would rather lower our tax liability and increase our cash flow by going with the cloud. Daryl, my controller, ran the numbers and we can apply the additional cash flow in other areas of the business to grow the company.

"Another thing we all like about Marie's solution relates to the cost savings of a cloud solution over an on-premise offering. It is the fact we are only paying for what we need. Cloud computing is a pay-as-you-go service. John did some analysis on our current servers to estimate how much of Bob's configuration we would actually use. He thinks it would only be about 10-20% of the server's capacity 80-90% of the time.

"Another issue for us is the longer implementation time adds cost to the project because we have unhappy customers and are losing opportunities to close new customers because our current system is causing so many problems. Accepting the longer implementation time of an on-premise solution could be very costly to us.

"One final note on cost: Experts say cloud computing is much friendlier on the environment because it uses less power than millions of small companies owning their own servers."

"So you're going to the cloud to save the world, is that it?" James joked.

"Hey, we're into meaningful work at our company," Esther shot back with a smile. "We welcome anything we can do to reinforce the fact our organization is making the world a better place." She then continued.

"The bottom line for us on cost is we prefer the cost savings and improved cash flow of a cloud solution. We both have quotes from Marie and Bob. Although you may differ with our choice of Marie's solution, is there anything I missed when considering the cost comparison of these two offerings?

"It may shock you," James began, "but my team basically agrees with you that economics is the primary motivation to go with the cloud. It is faster, simpler, and cheaper to use cloud applications. Implementations can be 20-50% faster. We can avoid the upfront capital required for servers, storage and software. There are no ongoing operational expenses for maintaining a server room and the equipment.

"Savings range from 20-90%, with simpler applications offering the highest savings. And as you mentioned, the tax benefits are not only attractive, they can provide significant opportunities to apply cash resources elsewhere in the organization to stimulate growth.

"I think you have it covered. We did come up with one idea that may be of interest to you. Have you considered a hybrid solution, where part is in the cloud and another part on-premise at your offices?"

"John mentioned it at one point, but going halfway is not my style," replied Esther.

"You don't have to tell us that," Peter responded with a light laugh.

"Don't get me wrong," Esther said in her defense. "We did fully consider it. We looked at which applications we would bring in-house and what would stay in the cloud, but it did not make sense to us. Marie's solution is tightly integrated for our needs. Maybe based on your objectives and needs, James, a hybrid solution may make sense. For us it does not."

"Okay, well I would like us to talk through the rest of our findings before I make my final decision," James replied. "What about scalability?"

Esther got back on track. "Our second responsibility was to evaluate **scalability**. I have great news. The scalability issues do not apply to firms our size. We studied elasticity in the cloud applications and both of our organizations fully comprehend scalability in on-premise solutions. Our problem has been software scalability. Our small business accounting program was great in the past, but we have outgrown it. As you have probably already concluded, the applications from Marie and Bob will scale with us easily.

"On-premise systems scale by adding equipment, software licenses, and getting bigger bandwidth. These are hard costs, take time, and may create some downtime, but we are both familiar with that process.

"On the other hand, cloud solutions scale as needed. They call it 'elasticity' in the cloud because it instantly scales as you need more computing power, bandwidth or storage.

"The fact is neither of our companies are retail, news or community websites that are going to go bonkers with tons of users visiting at once. Our scalability requirements are minimal compared to lots of other companies. We think the only scalability issue our companies will face in the next three years is purchasing additional user licenses. Therefore both Bob and Marie's solutions meet our scalability needs."

"I agree," added James. "We looked into this also, even though it was not our primary responsibility. It was just part of the information to consider. It's clear either of their software solutions will easily scale for our companies. The only issue is the licenses, and that relates more to cost or one of the other key areas we agreed to research."

"Our final key responsibility was **vendor viability**," Esther continued. "We rigorously interrogated each of them, researched their companies, talked with their references, and did everything we could to find fault with both of them. The good news is both appear to be great companies with reliable applications to meet our needs."

"We agree. Our findings are the same in those areas. It's just a question of cloud computing versus on-premise technology where we differ," James said. "So it appears at this stage, except for our technology preference, we're on the same page. Peter, do you think we overlooked anything?"

"I'm curious how deeply Esther considered a hybrid solution," Peter answered. "Certainly it's common for companies to outsource email and web hosting to the cloud. Does it make sense to possibly use a cloud solution for customer relationship management and keep your core accounting functionality in-house?"

"I left that discussion more to my team," admitted Esther. "John, who heads up our development, and Daryl, my controller, worked through the pros and cons of implementing a hybrid solution. You know me. I just want the bottom line. Their conclusion was it made more sense to implement all of our core business application needs in one tightly integrated solution. What about you, James? You're the one who brought it up."

"I think a hybrid solution along the lines of what Peter suggested has merit," replied James. "Initially I thought we might be able to run the new core business application on our existing servers and then access our email, website and customer relationship management in the cloud, which would save money. Unfortunately that would not work out. Our equipment should either be replaced now or within the next two years."

"That reminds me," Esther added. "One reason John and Daryl did <u>not</u> like a hybrid approach with the core applications is because the only companies they could find which had gone that way did so because of circumstances, rather than preference. I believe in each case they had existing servers and their software licenses were paid for one application, but their other core application licenses were expiring. They moved the applications that expired to the cloud and planned to replace the on-premise systems with cloud solutions when the licenses expired."

"Hmmm..." James replied thoughtfully, considering this new perspective. Privately, it was frustrating. He wanted to retain at least part of his solution in-house, but the facts were working against him.

"So what did you decide to do?" Esther demanded.

"I think I've made my decision, but I want to complete our conversation today first," James responded.

"So what did you find out?" Esther asked. Peter and James smiled at the way Esther was driving the conversation.

"Well, our primary responsibilities were to evaluate performance, reliability and security," James began. "**Performance** is clearly very strong in on-premise computing. I believe there are definitely situations where cloud computing can have slow access times, but based on our research these incidents are becoming far less common."

Esther was surprised to hear James conceding performance as an issue, but she knew to keep her mouth shut. James would want to go into detail. He continued.

"My IT guy, Travis, talked with users as well as the IT managers. The users either saw no performance difference in their on-premise applications or an improvement.

"I also contacted people to validate Bob's claims of superior performance and enthusiastic clients. I interviewed four of his clients. I asked a lot of questions and they all seem very pleased with Bob's company, their service and solutions.

"The performance issues for Bob's clients had more to do with the length of time it took them to implement their solutions. One client mentioned deadlines were missed, but in reality it was the client's fault. They had changed the specification for the system. Another client said there seemed to always be something to upgrade or improve.

"Of course, there was some downtime due to software upgrades to the servers. In one case a staff person caused an extended period of downtime because he installed a bunch of equipment incorrectly. In theory downtime due to software upgrades, equipment changes or employee errors are eliminated when you're in the cloud.

"Unfortunately for me, the conclusion of my team is Bob's clients are sticking with on-premise solutions because they're more comfortable with them rather than the applications are actually providing higher performance."

"Wow," said Esther. "Did it hurt to say that?"

"Honesty is more important than being right about something I said previously," James replied. "I still believe there are situations where cloud computing is going to be slower, but it appears Marie's Microsoft Dynamics solutions are quite competitive in the area of performance. Her references confirm it."

"Okay, so what about reliability? I notice you're saving security, which may be the hottest topic for last," asked Esther.

"Again, **reliability** is not a factor than significantly points us to the cloud or an on-premise solution," James admitted. "There have been outages at Amazon, Microsoft, Sony and the Goggle Blogger cloud services in the past, but if we want to be fair, then we have to admit on-premise solutions crash also. We each have to decide, in part, based on whether we believe these very large companies can manage their data centers better than we can manage our server rooms."

"So it really comes down to security, and your personal preference," suggested Peter. "Am I right?" James and Esther nodded, and then James continued.

"James, before we go on, I just want to say you are blowing me away. You always want proven solutions, tons of details, months to analyze the situation and often seem to prefer no decision to taking action," Esther complimented. "But today up to this point you seem to be very willing to consider whatever solution might be best."

"Esther, we've known each other for a long time," James began. "Don't think I have changed. I have been gathering information on alternative solutions for the past six months. I have talked with people at trade shows, contacted vendors, and done extensive research. The flexibility you perceive in my perspective developed from months of research and a commitment to respect the opinions of my team.

"Like you, I have a very competent management group. They knew my bias towards on-premise solutions going into this project and are well aware of our needs. I work with them to balance my preconceptions and analytical nature, just as you meet with me for casual accountability and to gather additional details you may be overlooking. Let me cover security and then let's get any other details on the table. After that I'll let you know my decision."

Go for it," Esther encouraged. Peter nodded for James to continue.

"**Security** is the biggest concern for both of our companies because the data in our systems is confidential to our clients as well as our organizations. I admit, at first Bob had me in his pocket on the security issue. This occurred in part because of my bias towards having the technology physically located in our offices.

"It's a bit dated, but there is an online statistic reported in USA Today on July 4, 2011 that between early 2008 and mid-2009 the number of cyber-attacks blocked by IBM's X-Force security division jumped from less than 10,000 to over 500,000 attacks a month. I'm sure this number is much higher today.

"This means small businesses like ours, particularly those serving the government, need to be experts at securing our systems. There are a growing number of attacks through the internet to private company server rooms to steal data, access bank accounts, or to take control of websites to run scams or infect other computers.

"The problem is neither of our companies are experts at internet security. I cannot speak for your people, but my team does not want to become one either. These attacks can be extremely difficult to detect and remove. If our servers became infected then our systems would be blocked and inaccessible. This could be for minutes, hours, days, or even weeks. It would be a real pain.

"The alternative is to put our faith in Microsoft's ability to protect their applications in the cloud. They have best-of-breed data centers that are SAS70 certified with the latest technology, firewalls and the highest possible levels of redundancy to give us multiple layers of defense. For us to try to replicate the security of their cloud offering would distract us from our core business. We do not have the time or the money to match their offering."

"So what you're saying," Peter suggested, "is there are risks implementing in the cloud as well as on-premise solutions. Am I correct?"

"Yes. I think the key in the cloud is to go with a very large provider like Microsoft as Marie is suggesting," James replied. "I do not trust the security capabilities of smaller hosting companies compared to larger companies with significant resources."

Esther was really surprised. James had worked on analyzing his options much earlier than she expected so he was ready to make a decision, and he was much more open to the cloud than she anticipated. She decided to throw the gauntlet down.

"So what if you could get a guarantee on performance, reliability, security, and vendor viability? Would you go with a cloud solution then?"

"What do you mean? We get to try out the cloud and if we don't like it for any reason we can move to an on-premise solution? James was skeptical.

"Yes," Esther replied confidently. "Let's say you implement in the cloud. For whatever reason, six months down the road you hate it. Here's what you can do with Marie's solution: Microsoft allows you to transfer your database from the cloud to an on-premise installation. Since you only paid to rent the software from Microsoft, there isn't a credit, but you can implement your on-premise version more quickly. It's basically a no-risk trial period. You can't lose!"

"Are you sure the data is usable," Peter questioned.

"Marie assures us, and showed us confirmation from Microsoft, that the data can be transferred to an on-premise system," Esther replied. "There are some companies offering cloud solutions that do _not_ give you your data in a useable fashion. Once you go off their system, you have no access or you have to download raw data files to import into a new system as best you can. But that's not Marie and Microsoft. They support us either way."

There was a pause in the conversation as James considered this new information. Peter spoke first.

"Esther, it sounds like you are going with Marie's solution. As you say, you see no risk. What do you believe our non-profit should do?"

"For similar reasons as ours, I think you should go with Marie's cloud solution," Esther replied, surprising no one. "It lowers your upfront costs, eliminates your need for additional in-house or contract staffing, and will resolve your issues faster. And, as I just explained, if it turns out the cloud is not right for you then you can move to an on-premise system."

Peter nodded, and they both looked at James, who took a deep breath and sighed.

"I understand the cost of trying a cloud solution for six months, if we wanted to take Microsoft up on their guarantee," James explained. "I admit we were stuck in a cloud versus on-premise thought pattern. Our compromise position was the hybrid one, but you bring up a good point why that may be flawed. Even with a hybrid solution our first year costs are substantially higher and it stretches out the implementation timeframe.

"I like Microsoft's offer and Marie has been very impressive. My team prefers her cloud solution. I like piloting something with potential, rather than locking ourselves into an expensive on-premise system, because then we can make changes if necessary. We don't have that flexibility with the Bob's solution. We would be locked in. Wow..." James' voice trailed off and he shook his head slightly. There was a pause as Peter and Esther gave James a moment to think.

"My decision is to join you both in going with Marie's cloud solution," stated James with growing confidence.

Esther did not resist the opportunity to chide James about his decision. "I know you like the ability to pilot Microsoft's solution in the cloud, but the real reason you're going with Marie is because you're worried if you don't, then my company is going to grow much faster than yours. While you would be wallowing in on-premise costs and a delayed implementation, my company would be growing like gangbusters. You just couldn't live with that, could you?"

"Actually through this process we learned some ways to grow much more rapidly," James countered with a broad smile. "In the next three years we are going to leave your company way, way behind. You're going to be sucking dust and begging me for advice on how to catch-up with us. Enjoy your smug moment. Remember, I'm already planning ahead."

"Wanna bet?" Esther challenged.

"Yes, I do," Peter interjected. Esther and James turned to him. "My team has also learned a lot from this process. We have identified some things we were doing that wasted tons of time and caused lost opportunities to grow our organization to help more people. We have confirmed 17 ways to leverage this new system to accelerate our growth. I bet our rate of growth will be faster than either of your companies, or I'll buy you and your spouses' dinner at the restaurant of your choice."

James and Esther laughed. "You're on," replied Esther.

"Count me in," said James. "This is an interesting turn of events."

"Yep, and time to go," Esther agreed. "Thanks, gentlemen, for everything. I'll see you at our next board meeting, if not speak with you before then. Right now I've got to see a woman about an ERP solution."

"I already texted her about meeting tomorrow," James said. "So don't think you're getting started before me."

"No problem," Esther said as she grabbed her coated and turned to leave. "I scheduled my meeting to sign our contract with her days ago. It starts in 30 minutes. Have fun, guys!" She waved and happily walked out of the coffee shop.

Chapter 30

What's

Changed

In a word, the internet is becoming ubiquitous, which is a big word for "reliable, available anywhere, and fast." For instance, the major U.S. airlines are offering online access onboard a growing number of flights and more carriers are promising access soon.

The IT model for the past decade has been local servers managed by internal IT staff. And business thrived! It is a rare company that did not follow this model. However, when we look closely at this strategy, there are many limitations.

- IT staff are expensive and technology is difficult to manage.
- It costs more to cool and power on-premise servers than their original cost.
- On-premise servers typically run at 10-20 percent of capacity.
- Technology updates for hardware and software are expensive.

Today, the IT department represents a significant cost for many businesses. The investment in servers and IT staff continues to grow and equipment is purchased to meet the peak needs that occur only rarely.

Now there is a new breed of business emerging. They don't have on-premise servers and their IT staff is minimal. They leverage data centers to share server power and utilize the IT talents of the center. They have no capital tied up in computer equipment (other than what is on their desks) and the savings they experience are substantial. Every firm is different, but the cost savings can be an eye opener.

Even firms that retain ownership of IT staff and equipment are using virtualization to reduce the number of servers. For example, the CTO of a mid-sized company reduced the number of servers from 120 to 20 and eventually plans to have 10 servers running many virtual sessions with much greater utilization. Firms that do not use virtualization technology are wasting money on outdated equipment.

Early cloud adopters found they could make these significant improvements by changing their IT strategy. Here are some examples:

- Reduced IT staff costs, as companies can often save $100,000 or more annually for each employee that is no longer required.

- Hardware capital costs are eliminated and replaced by monthly expenses.

- Servers in the cloud are more fully utilized.

- Firms are going green by virtualizing servers in the cloud.

- Additional processors and storage can be assigned as needed.

- Server management is handled by data center staff and monitoring is automated.

- Security is actually improved in the data center.

Like most business trends, cost savings are driving the rapid adoption of cloud computing. Not for profit firms, like the one featured in our fable are a good example. The challenge of raising new funds has driven many of these organizations to the cloud to reduce their administrative expenses and put more resources into their primary mission.

Imagine the ways your business could use the money saved when you move your core software applications to the cloud.

Chapter 31

Indicators You Need

ERP

A start-up is a beautiful thing. Communications are easy due to the small number of staff, customer relationships are personal, and billing is straightforward, often done with a word processor or spreadsheet program.

Then comes success. More staff, more customers. One day, your firm is doing business with customers the owner has never met. Accounting becomes the responsibility of someone else, and eventually a team of experienced accountants is hired.

Soon thereafter your firm has to present numbers to a bank or an investor. A client asks a complex billing question that requires organized records and quick access. Employees need access to inventory, accounts receivable and vendor information. Government contractors need to be compliant with audit requirements to bid on contracts.

This usually happens somewhere between $2 million and $10 million in gross sales – with typically between 10 and 25 employees. At some point, a business starts to feel substantial pain and growth is restricted.

Organizations in this position have two accounting system options:

1. **On-premise system**: Purchase a server, upgrade workstations, buy software and hire an experienced firm to help implement the software and train the

employees. The cost is paid over the term of the project, usually two to six months. Existing or new IT staff manages the system, provides backup, and maintains the servers.

2. **Cloud system**: For a monthly fee, your firm has access to servers and software in a secure data center. Implementation is much the same as on-premise and some firms include services in the monthly fee. No new IT staff required and capital is preserved to grow the business. The system is accessible both from the office and remotely.

The bottom line is the growth of your firm is limited unless the combination of your accounting systems and staff are up to the job.

A new ERP system should support your firm's growth for a number of years. The system should efficiently scale as you expand without requiring you to add significant accounting staff.

Some of the key indicators your ERP system is successfully deployed are self-service portals, universal access to critical data, a strong security model, and flexible reporting.

As your firm grows, future enhancements address changes in the organization's pain points. These capabilities might include document management and work flow approvals, web integrations, automated banking, and integrated Customer Relationship Management (sales to accounting interface). There are many other options available and your ERP should have easy integration points for add-on, third-party products.

The following are indications your organization needs an ERP system. Ask yourself these questions:

- ❑ Is our current system slow?

- ❑ Are people locked-out of our system until other users log-out because our accounting software cannot support more users?

- ❑ Has generating reports in Excel or Access become cumbersome, time consuming, prone to mistakes, and frustrating?

- ❑ Is doing the reports manually fully meeting your needs?

- ❑ Are there a lot of manual processes necessary to close out service tickets, projects, payroll, company financial reporting, and other important business tasks?

- ❑ Does data have to be entered twice because we have disconnected systems?

Here are additional questions to ask about your business to confirm your organization need to upgrade to an ERP system:

- ❑ Is information incomplete or not available when we need it to support decisions?

- ❑ Are our revenues growing?

- ❑ Are we are hiring more employees?

- ❑ Are we having trouble keeping track of spreadsheets with accounting-related or financial data?

- ❑ Are departments not working efficiently or effectively together because they lack the financial data from each other?

- ❑ Is it difficult to forecast or plan?

- ❑ Is our current system more than five years old?

- ❑ Is our current system not meeting our functional needs?

- ❏ Does our current system not integrate and/or not allow the import/export of data with other third-party products?

- ❏ Are there not enough contact management fields/capabilities in our current system to meet our needs?

- ❏ Is it difficult to pass audits because our system does not fully meet all the requirements?

- ❏ Is it difficult to pass tax and/or financial audits because so much data is being managed manually?

- ❏ Is expensive customization the only way to get more from our current system?

- ❏ Are we approaching or have exceeded the capacity for information that can be maintained in the database of our current system?

- ❏ Are we concerned about security and therefore want our accounting software more proactively managed and backed-up regularly.

- ❏ Do we want improved redundancy/failover capability, and better protection from hackers?

- ❏ Do the people supporting our system respond slowly to our needs?

- ❏ Are our internal IT resources expensive and seem to grow each year?

Chapter 32

Questions
To Ask About An ERP Solution

ERP systems offer growing organizations significant benefits:

1. Your business data and applications become centralized for easier, real-time access. This gives you access to information on company profitability and productivity across all divisions and departments.

2. A single integrated ERP system eliminates the need for duplicate data entry.

3. ERP scales with your organization rather than slowing you down.

4. Training is faster, easier and less costly when you use Microsoft Dynamics ERP solutions because in many ways it looks-and-feels like Microsoft Office.

5. A great ERP system runs on a reliable computing platform and provides a stable and secure environment. This is particularly true with Microsoft Dynamics hosted cloud solutions where the resources of the data center protect your data's security.

6. Flexible reporting options are one of the most important benefits of an ERP system. You can extract and utilize critical data to make better decisions,

customize reports, and utilize dashboards to quickly view the health of your organization.

7. Perhaps most important, your staff can serve clients faster, more comprehensively, and with less errors because your ERP system provides more real-time client data than they have today.

You probably have a list of specific problems, needs and/or desires related to your business that are driving you to consider an ERP solution as an upgrade to QuickBooks or another business accounting system. Every situation is unique.

We suggest asking seven key questions of ERP software vendors or their VARs to confirm how well their solutions and service help you achieve your objectives. Use the questions that best apply to your situation.

1. **References**: What is your experience implementing ERP for companies like ours?

   Ideally you want to obtain:

   a. A list of companies similar to yours that are currently using their ERP software.

   b. Demonstrated competence and understanding of your organization's needs based on serving similar clients. If they are truly skilled at serving firms in your industry, then during your interviews they should ask you relevant questions and suggest ways to improve upon your current processes.

      ACTION: Ask each VAR for demonstrations of their ERP software implemented at similar companies. Here are three questions to ask their clients that may help you:

1. Did the implementation meet your expectations and how has support been since the go-live date of the new system?

2. In what ways has the software enabled your firm to achieve more with the same (or fewer) number of people?

3. What are the five biggest problems you and your employees solved with the new software?

2. **ERP Software Options**: There are two areas to consider here to make certain you have limited your risks:

   a. Does each VAR offer both on-premise and cloud versions of their software? If yes, can you transfer the database from one platform to the other?

   b. If you decide not to discontinue using the software, can you get your information out in a format that easily imports into another solution?

   ACTION: Ask for a demonstration of how these processes are performed.

3. **Time**: These questions concern the timeframe for implementing the solution you choose.

   a. How long will it take to go live on the software?

   b. How much time is included in your project costs to support post-go live activities?

   c. How much time will our employees need to commit on a weekly basis and for how long to support the project and to learn the new system?

d. How will each VAR manage the project – in the areas of communications, budget status, open items lists, time frame status, etc.?

e. Will the VAR assign a Project Manager to the project and what is the process used?

   ACTION: Confirm a clear schedule with each VAR, and determine how long implementations took at similar companies they provided as references.

f. **Costs:** What are the total costs of the solution, including software, hardware and implementation? Consider these factors;

   o Cloud solutions typically have only a monthly subscription fee whereas on-premise software has a license, maintenance and possibly other fees involved. Confirm you are being quoted <u>all costs</u>. Include everyone who needs access. There are two pricing options;

   ✓ *User-based pricing:* One license fee per user to access all modules.

   ✓ *Module-based pricing:* Buy the modules you need on an a la carte basis, plus smaller per user fees.

   NOTE: There are *concurrent users* (maximum number of people on the software at a time) or *named users* (anyone with a license can access the software simultaneously):

   o Integrations

   o Custom development or configuration

   o Upgrades

- o Guaranteed compatibility with future versions

- o Annual maintenance

- o Term commitment – length of contract?

Hardware (for on-premise systems):

- o Servers

- o Other hardware such as hard drives, monitors, racks...

- o Non-ERP application software, such as the server operating system, database, security software...

- o Networking cables, switches...

g. <u>Taxes</u>: Are you depreciating the costs of the on-premise system over many years, or subscribing to a cloud solution that is 100% tax-deductible as payments are made? Does each VAR offer the payment option you prefer?

h. <u>Other Costs</u>:

- o Project planning, project management, implementation and testing

- o Data conversion

- o Third party add-on products

- o Training

- o Tech support

- o Services: What is the hourly rate for work outside the scope of the project?

- o Internal staff time

- o Facilities, heating/air conditioning, physical security, furniture, maintenance... to house any equipment

- o The rate for hourly service beyond the scope of this project

- o Ask: What have we left out that needs to be included?

i. <u>Other Considerations</u>:

- o What are the conditions for the final payment?

- o How are billing questions handled?

ACTION: Ask each VAR if any other factors need to be considered. Request the full costs of both cloud and on-premise platforms in-writing. Compare the final costs to your organization for each platform.

4. **Security and Remote Access**: Ask each VAR for a detailed explanation of how data is encrypted to make it secure. Determine how your staff will access data from anywhere they are working.

For instance, you may have project managers who need to remotely access your ERP system for project/task creation, editing, resource assignment, budgeting, time/expense entry and approval, and real-time analysis of their projects.

Or you may need tighter security rules to comply with Sarbanes-Oxley requirements so your firm passes accounting audits. This may involve a combination of password rules such as maximum/minimum lengths, character types (uppercase, lowercase, numbers, special characters), password expiration by time, automatic requirements for users to change their passwords and more.

> **ACTION**: Ask each VAR for a demonstration of how people can access data from any location. Make certain your security and remote access requirements are clear and each VAR finalist meets them completely.

5. **Flexibility**: Where are the areas where you need the software to adapt to your company's specific needs?

   > **ACTION**: Ask each VAR for examples of how their ERP software was configured at companies similar to yours. Confirm the software is flexible enough to meet all of your needs.

6. **Business Continuity**: Confirm the VAR's Physical location (including hardware and software), back-up systems, and disaster recovery processes meet your needs. Every on-premise and cloud site is going to have some downtime. The question is, how much? Ask:

   a. What happens if our company cannot access our data for any reason?

   b. How often are files backed-up?

   c. How long does it take to restore files that are backed-up?

   d. How much downtime can be expected for scheduled maintenance and upgrades?

   e. How far in advance do you communicate maintenance notices, outage issues, or fixes?

   f. Are there any types of downtime where we are not notified in advance?

g. What hours can we reach your technical support team, by what methods and what is your guaranteed response time?

ACTION: Ask these questions of each VAR, and possibly request a site visit, references of clients that were restored after downtime, or a demonstration of restoring data.

Chapter 33

Questions

To Ask Your Technology Partner

The people designing, implementing, and supporting your solution are <u>more important</u> than the ERP software you choose. These questions apply whether your ERP solution is being designed, implemented and supported by a software manufacturer or a local technology partner (VAR).

It is important to work with an experienced team that properly analyzes your business requirements, recommends ways to streamline operations, and fully understands how to configure the system to meet your unique needs. Yes, even though other companies in your industry use the solution, most organizations feel they have "unique" needs.

Our understanding is that 90 percent of ERP customers buy from a local resource. While this may drop a bit with the emergence of cloud applications, you need to determine if it is important for you to meet and work directly with a local solution provider.

Here are some important questions for any partner:

1. **Company Information**: These questions help you to understand their experience with ERP and in serving clients with organizations similar to yours:

    ACTION: Ask these questions and confirm details as necessary:

a. How long has your company been implementing ERP solutions?

b. What is the experience of the consultants who will be working on this project?

c. Is your implementation team located in this area (particularly important for on-premise solutions)?

d. Are you a reseller for a manufacturer, or do you manufacture this solution?

e. Where is your data center (cloud) located?

f. Is your data center SAS70 certified?

g. How many customers have you deployed (cloud/on-premise)?

h. Will the project have a dedicated project manager or will the consulting team handle these tasks? (Hint: You want a dedicated project manager.)

i. How is support handled after the initial implementation?

j. Do you have a dedicated help desk or is this function handled by the implementation staff?

k. What is the typical response time of your help desk?

l. Who is my contact with your management team after the implementation is complete?

2. **Industry Expertise:** You want your local resource to have experience serving clients at similar organizations.

   ACTION: Ask to speak with and visit companies in your industry for which the local partner has provided similar ERP solutions (not other types of firms or software). It is best for the reference sites to be companies of a similar size that implemented projects of a similar scope as yours. Here are some suggestions to consider:

a. You can ask questions similar to the ones above to determine the industry expertise of a VAR. See first-hand how their clients are using the solution.

b. Talk with others beyond the key contact at each client reference site to consider different real-world experiences of deploying, customizing, and working with the solution. This might include IT staff, department managers, and end users in various office roles.

c. Develop a professional relationship with at least one contact so you can share experiences moving forward.

3. **Background**: You are going to depend on this partner, so complete a full due diligence. Well-run companies are open with information to help you comprehend the true character of their organization and principals, whereas less reputable firms often provide unspecific responses and have questionable data that becomes evident during your research.

   ACTION: Follow these steps to confirm the background of the partner:

a. Check with your professional network to see if anyone has done business with the company or knows the founders.

b. Search for their company on the Better Business Bureau website, Yelp.com and any other customer opinion websites. Keep in mind that we all have at least one past or even current client that is not satisfied with our company. *Sometimes it is a problem with the client.* Try to balance being fair with discerning the truth when considering comments from unhappy clients.

c. Since the technology partner will have access to your proprietary technology, customer records, financial, and other confidential information, you should work through David's company, www.SuccessWithPeople.com/background-checks/ or another partner to do a background check on the company <u>and</u> its principal officers. This is cheap insurance and a critical step designed to protect your business and limit your liability. We recommend you complete a thorough background check before signing any contract to implement your ERP solution.

d. Request their company history and discuss it with them. Try to discern whether their story is true or exaggerated in any way.

e. Ask for copies of their mission statement, company values, vision statement, and any other documents pertaining to their company culture. This provides insights into how they respond to problems when you work together – *and there will be bumps in the road with <u>every</u> project, or else you would not need them in the first place.*

f. Some organizations at contract time like to ask for a copy of the partner company's financials. This may be too much to ask of private companies. If you ask good questions of their clients and do the other checks above then you should gain a reasonable assessment of their financial condition.

4. **Demo**: Make the most of your demo. Software demonstrations are designed to make the product look good. The key is to make the partner adapt their demo to your specific needs.

> **ACTION**: Prepare a series of real-life scenarios that are critical to your organization that you want the ERP solution to handle. Provide these to the partner in advance and ask them to demonstrate how their solution manages these situations. They may not be able to show you every scenario, but they should be able to explain how the software meets your needs in ways you understand.

5. **Support & Training**: Technology is not always easy to use, maintain or keep operating. This is why you need a solid technology partner to support your company and train your people on how to make the most of your ERP investment.

> **ACTION**: Consider these steps to ascertain the quality of support and training that will be offered by your partner:

    a. Include questions about support and training as part of your reference check in #1 above.

    b. Ask for a demonstration of their support system. Perhaps the VAR will let you listen in as one of their clients contacts the partner for support.

    c. Ask for a demonstration of the training, or to participate in a training with another client.

6. **Test Drive**: Having the ability to try the software for 30-60 days gives you the most realistic experience possible. This is one reason cloud solutions are preferred in many cases. It is easy to test a cloud ERP

solution and experience the partner or VAR's support, even if you have to pay for the test drive.

> **ACTION**: Ask for a test drive or trail period. Many partners have demo sites you can try out. The ideal situation would be a trial period rather than a test drive so you can use the work entered during your "test drive" should you decide to move forward with the purchase. Please note: It may be a shrewd investment for you to pay for some basic training to get the most from your test drive.

Bill Thanks...

One day in 1983, a colleague stopped by with a request. "I have a friend that needs some help with a computer inventory program," she explained. "Can you help them?" As they say, things progressed from there.

I'd like to extend a heartfelt thanks to the SSi employees for their dedication to making clients successful. We have a great team. I especially want to thank our management team, Jeff Vonasek and Mike McNeese (co-owners of SSi Consulting both of whom have more than 20 years' experience implementing ERP software), Suzy Zgorski (for believing Project Management could change our company), Karen Riordan (for letting me think I'm coaching her in selling) and Paula Vonasek (one of the smartest CPA's I know). If we succeed in any way, it is all due to our outstanding team.

Horses are my passion. I spent a year trying to help my mare, Willow, do a nice round circle. She tried everything but round just never occurred to her. One day, she did a pretty circle with ease. When I asked what had changed, she said 'If I had known that was what you wanted, I would have done it long ago.' Thanks to The Kindred Spirit, Willow, Peanut and Little Bits for teaching me patience and for bringing so much joy into my life.

And thanks to my wife of 32 years, Patricia, for all her suggestions and comments on this book. You are in here too.

David Thanks...

Although my life has been blessed with success, I have also had to learn a lot the hard way due to my mistakes. I am very grateful to Jesus for giving me hope when times have been dark, an opportunity to leave the past behind and a never-ending stream of opportunity.

I am very thankful for Terry, my wife of 34 years, for challenging me, staying with me through the tough times, and loving me. Our children are also a special blessing in our lives. Luke, Jeff and Jennylin came first as our biological children. Arie joined us in 2001 when he was 10 years old and is now off on his own. Aaliyah, Myah, Izaiah and Izabellah (ages 2-7) joined us in April 2011. The similarities between raising children and leading people continue to amaze me.

Our Clients are AWESOME – so THANK YOU! Our company exists to serve you. My thanks to Bill for inspiring this book so it serves people considering moving beyond small business accounting software and spreadsheets to ERP. Last, but not least, a very special thank you to key members of the Success With People team, particularly David Reyes for his design help.

William S. Aiton

Bill is president of <u>SSi Consulting</u> a firm specializing in Microsoft cloud and on-premise accounting/ERP solutions for small and mid-size businesses. Bill has been helping businesses successfully select and implement computerized accounting solutions to improve productivity for more than 25 years. A graduate of the University of Virginia, he completed his MBA in Accounting from the University of Tennessee. In 1983 he founded Business Computer Solutions, an accounting software solution firm that became one of the top 20 resellers for Microsoft Dynamics™ SL (Solomon) in the U.S. In 1997 he sold his company and became one of the founding partners of LBMC Technologies located in Nashville, Tennessee.

In his eight years as a partner of SSi Consulting, he has focused the firm on Microsoft Dynamics™ GP (Great Plains), and Microsoft Dynamics™ SL (Solomon) , positioning the company in the top 5% of accounting software resellers. In 2009, Microsoft selected SSi Consulting as Mid-Atlantic Partner of the Year.

He and companies he has led have received numerous awards including, Microsoft Dynamics™ SL (Solomon) Software Customer Service Award, Microsoft Dynamics™ SL (Solomon) Software Top Regional Salesperson Award, the Ron Herring Mission of Service Award from the Mankind Project. SSi has been a member of the Microsoft Partner Advisory Council and the Microsoft SL Product Advisory board. Bill helped to found the Microsoft Center of Excellence for Government Contractors and the Microsoft Center of Excellence for Not for Profits, both located in Washington DC.

David Russell

David Russell is CEO of Success With People, where his team trains and coaches entrepreneurs to develop a powerful company culture that provides a sustainable competitive advantage. Services include coaching, consulting, hiring/ employee assessments, motivational speaking, peer groups Best Tech Workplace surveys and programs to train companies how to deliver a more consistent superior customer experience.

He is also CEO of MANAGEtoWIN, an integrated, very low cost, online talent management portal that helps motivate people to be more productive, profitable and personally fulfilled in their careers with your company.

David has authored and co-authored five books. He has directly served over 200 organizations during the last three years. His career in the computer industry began in 1982. As a consultant, coach or speaker he has served Microsoft, Cisco, Intel, Tech Data, Ingram Micro, Autotask, ConnectWise, Tigerpaw, Catalyst Telecom, CompTIA, Heartland Technology Groups, Everything Channel, InsideNGO, Vistage and Entrepreneur's Organization members.

To learn more about David and his companies' services visit:

www.SuccessWithPeople.com

www.MANAGEtoWIN.com

www.ssiconsulting.com

Why should you trust SSi Consulting? We encourage you to ask Microsoft and our customers.

Microsoft named SSi Consulting as 2009 Partner of the Year for the mid-Atlantic. Our customers are showcased by Microsoft case studies on its website. SSi serves on Microsoft's SL Product Advisory Board where we bring the needs of our customers directly to Microsoft product developers.

Those are just a few compelling reasons to trust SSi Consulting's people, process and products. Here are a few more:

- Founded in 1983 - more than 27 years of experience

- Serving 300+ clients from offices located in Columbia, Maryland and McLean, Virginia

- Expert teams of CPAs, consultants, systems engineers and project managers

- A collaborative working style that values honest communication

Don't take our word for it; hear what current customers have to say. Contact us today to learn more.

- **Methodology**: We have dedicated project managers to guide your project to a successful, on time and on budget completion.

- **Leadership**: Our management team has deep leadership experience. See our bios online for additional information.

- **Recognition**: Some of our awards include: Microsoft Dynamics Mid-Atlantic Partner of the Year, Accounting Technology Magazine Top 100 Value Added Reseller (VAR) Technology Pacesetter Award, and the Baltimore Business Journal Top 25 List of IT Consulting Firms.

- **Career Opportunities**: SSi Consulting is a healthy, growing company with an entrepreneurial spirit. You can build a bright future with us.

www.SSiConsulting.com • info@ssiconsulting.com

410-944-3369

SUCCESS WITH PEOPLE

"We increased our billable hours by 240 hours in one month by implementing what we learned from Success With People."

Chris Pickard, COO, Xylotek Solutions

Success With People services help you better engage your company's greatest assets – your employees – so they take more responsibility for delivering a consistently superior client experience.

Here is a brief overview of our services.

Background Checks

Online background checks – *never hire without doing a background check!*

Best Tech Workplaces

Confidential survey for IT solution providers to benchmark employee engagement with peers.

Company Culture Challenge

Community with optional training, coaching and benchmarking to help you develop a better company culture and superior client experience.

Coaching & Consulting

Designed to help you more quickly apply *The Company Culture Challenge* in your firm based on your unique needs.

Hire The Best	Comprehensive, contract recruitment program to help you hire great people instead of actors.
MANAGEtoWIN	Low-cost, easy-to-use talent management software to help you fully engage your people.
Professional Speaking	Engaging, fun, motivational keynotes, breakouts and workshops that give your people content they can apply in your firm.
Talent Assessments	Improve how your people work together and identify truly top performing team members in your hiring process by understanding their true behaviors & values.

www.SuccessWithPeople.com ◆ info@successwithpeople.com

(877) 514-0200 x200

Also by David Russell

How To Guides

The Company Culture Challenge

Hire The Best Avoid The Rest

Success With People

40 Days to Success With People

Business Fables

The EHR Guru

References

[1] Agility and innovation in delivering new apps emerging as key cloud adoption drivers, Mark Cox, eChannelLine, June 26, 2011, http://www.echannelline.com/usa/story.cfm?item=26936 (viewed June 27, 2011).

[2] New cyberattacks target small businesses, Byron Acohido, USA TODAY, http://www.usatoday.com/money/smallbusiness/2011-07-04-small-business-cyber-attackss_n.htm (viewed July 7, 2011).